Mergers and Acquisitions

Praise for *Mergers and Acquisitions*

"Several years ago, I moderated an executive forum on M&As at Forbes in New York. We examined a range of issues faced by executives as they engaged in M&As. Jeff served on a panel of executives that discussed the 'soft side' of merger integration. At that time, Jeff was working with Walt Shill at Accenture to develop new insights on executive turnover and the negative impact that leadership instability has on merger effectiveness. This book presents new perceptions from Jeff's years of research in the area. I highly recommend it to executives involved in the merger integration process."

—Neil Weinberg, Executive Editor, Forbes

"Jeff Krug and I may be considered fellow travelers. We have both long been interested in the top management turnover effects of M&As. However, any comparison stops right there. While I was interested in how such turnover might increase our understanding of corporate control practices, Jeff knew that it was about so much more. He knew that managing turnover is crucial to a firm's ability to unlock value in corporate control changes. This book is a wonderful testament to his insight . . . and to his dogged determination to fully understand how top management team dynamics can either ensure a combination's success or doom it to failure. Academics and executives alike will really appreciate his mastery of these issues."

—James P. Walsh, Carey Professor of Management
Ross School of Business, University of Michigan

"I approached Jeff a few years ago about his research on executive turnover in M&As after reading his article in *Harvard Business Review*. His research validated my experience with the tumultuous effects of M&As on top management teams. These I had witnessed while working with many clients over the years. We have since worked together to discover new insights into post-merger leadership issues. These efforts have helped Accenture support clients during merger integration work. I highly recommend this book to executives involved in M&As."

—Walt Shill, Global Managing Director, Accenture LLC

"Dr. Krug is nationally recognized for his research on M&As and its effects on top management. His recent article on executive churn following M&As is one of the most popular papers recently published in the *Journal of Business Strategy*. This book expands on this topic and provides a practical framework to show acquiring firms how they can retain the most effective executives in both companies. Executives, consultants, and academics alike will find Dr. Krug's research valuable, readable, and insightful."

—Nanci Healy, Editor, *Journal of Business Strategy*

Mergers and Acquisitions

Turmoil in Top Management Teams

Jeffrey A. Krug

Mergers and Acquisitions: Turmoil in Top Management Teams
Copyright © Business Expert Press, LLC, 2009.

First published in 2009 by
Business Expert Press, LLC
222 East 46th Street, New York, NY 10017
www.businessexpertpress.com

ISBN-13: 978-1-60649-056-3 (paperback)
ISBN-10: 1-60649-056-7 (paperback)

ISBN-13: 978-1-60649-057-0 (e-book)
ISBN-10: 1-60649-057-5 (e-book)

DOI 10.4128/9781606490570

A publication in the Business Expert Press Strategic Management collection

Collection ISSN: 2150-9611 (print)
Collection ISSN: 2150-9646 (electronic)

Cover design by Artistic Group—Monroe, NY
Interior design by Scribe, Inc.

First edition: December 2009

10 9 8 7 6 5 4 3 2 1

Printed in the United States of America.

For Alan and Viviane

Abstract

Mergers and acquisitions (M&As) can be tumultuous for executives. Target companies can expect to lose close to 40% of their top management teams within 2 years after an acquisition. Executives who stay often lose status and autonomy and view their company's acquisition as detrimental to themselves, both personally and professionally.

It is common for acquiring firms to replace target executives with their own shortly after an acquisition. Existing research, however, suggests that doing so leads to lower target company performance. Why, then, are acquiring firms so quick to replace target company executives after an acquisition?

Mergers and Acquisitions: Turmoil in Top Management Teams gives executives an in-depth look at the consequences of M&As for acquired top management teams. It examines M&As as a corporate growth strategy, the importance of top management teams to a firm's long-term performance, the reasons why executives depart after an acquisition, and the effects of these departures on target company performance. It then discusses when executive turnover may be desirable or undesirable and how acquiring firms can more effectively manage target company executive teams during the integration process.

An understanding of these leadership issues may play an important role in determining merger success.

Keywords

Mergers and acquisitions, top management teams, executive leadership, executive turnover, cross-border acquisitions

Contents

Preface

During the mid-1980s, I was a manager at PepsiCo, Inc. PepsiCo's corporate strategy was to build a strong market position in three industry groups: (a) soft drinks, (b) snack foods, and (c) restaurants. PepsiCo's restaurant division included Kentucky Fried Chicken (KFC), Taco Bell, and Pizza Hut. In 1988—less than 2 years after PepsiCo's acquisition of KFC in October 1986—I joined KFC as manager of finance and strategic planning. My responsibilities included managing KFC's monthly financial reporting documents, which were presented to the president of KFC-International each month. I also managed the strategic planning process, analyzed potential acquisitions, and presented proposals for new restaurant construction projects in Puerto Rico, Mexico, and Venezuela—where our three Latin American subsidiaries were based—to our president.

Shortly after I joined KFC, a rumor spread throughout KFC's headquarters that a PepsiCo executive—who was visiting KFC for the day—was overheard in the cafeteria saying, "There will be no more homegrown tomatoes in this organization." KFC employees were noticeably upset. A number of terminations of established KFC executives followed—the personnel director, general counsel, and controller, among others. Despite the fact that the acquisition had occurred 2 years earlier, the organization appeared to be in a continuous state of turmoil. One employee told me that more KFC employees were seeking psychological counseling for stress than at any time in the history of the organization. A PepsiCo executive remarked to me that "We're a performance organization. You might have been a star last year but if you don't perform this year, you're gone. There are a hundred executives with Ivy League MBAs back in PepsiCo headquarters who would love to have your job."

As a PepsiCo employee, I'm certain that I didn't feel the same stress that longer-tenured KFC employees probably felt, although I was plenty stressed. We worked 12-hour days, 6 and a half days each week. There were times when I worked all night to meet deadlines. I became good friends with many KFC employees, many of whom were born and raised in Louisville and had been with KFC for many years. The anxiety and stress they felt was apparent. Many did not know whether they would have a job when they walked in the next morning—and I knew several who did walk into work only to be told that they had been terminated. PepsiCo employees referred to Colonel Sanders as the "Old Man." The Colonel, however, was revered by people in Louisville. He was paternalistic and cared for his employees. There was a lot of loyalty to him. The cultural divide between PepsiCo executives from New York and KFC employees from Louisville was an important reason why the acquisition never worked. PepsiCo divested its restaurants in 1997.

I left PepsiCo to pursue my doctorate in strategy and international business at Indiana University in the late 1980s. My experience at PepsiCo and KFC motivated me to conduct research on the effects of acquisitions on target company executives following mergers and acquisitions (M&As). This book represents the result of almost 20 years of research in this area to date. It summarizes what we know about the level of turnover that occurs among executive ranks following an acquisition and the reasons why executives leave. It discusses M&As as a corporate growth strategy and why so many M&As fail. It examines the link between executive turnover and postmerger performance. Finally, it provides a road map for executives and consultants that can be used to analyze M&As, create strategies for dealing with top management team issues, and maximize integration success.

Richmond, Virginia
August 2009

CHAPTER 1

Turmoil in Top Management Teams Following Mergers and Acquisitions

Out of a corporate office of 126, only six were offered positions—the rest became history. The company for the most part has since been broken apart and sold.

—Chairman of the board shortly after his company was acquired in a hostile takeover by a corporate raider

The Role of Top Management Teams

A firm's top management team is composed of its top executives—those responsible for formulating and executing strategies for achieving the firm's long-term goals and creating sustainable competitive advantage. Strategy making has become an increasingly difficult—and important— task given globalization trends and rapid technological change over the last 30 years. Globalization trends have subjected firms to more intense competition from multinational firms with global scale advantages, global suppliers with greater negotiating power, and a wider range of customers located worldwide who have differing product and brand loyalties. Technology trends have increased the costs of developing new technologies and shortened product life cycles. To cover escalating costs, many firms have turned to global markets as a means of expanding sales volume. In sum, globalization trends and technological change have made it increasingly difficult for executives to sustain high levels of performance over the long term. Among their many responsibilities, executives are responsible for the following:

- *Determining the firm's mission.* A mission is the firm's reason for being. In what businesses should the firm compete? What customer needs should be served? What competencies are necessary for meeting customer needs? The mission may also outline the organization's values—those things that define the character of the organization and its employees. Establishing the firm's mission is an important task because it establishes boundaries for executives' actions. A narrowly defined mission can protect shareholder interests by discouraging executives from undertaking risky ventures or diversifying into businesses unrelated to the firm's core competencies. However, it can also unnecessarily hamper executives as they respond to maturing markets, technology changes, and industry turbulence.

- *Establishing a corporate vision.* The vision describes what the firm wants to become. Similar to the "BHAG" concept (big, hairy, audacious goals) described by Jim Collins in his book *Good to Great*, executives are responsible for visionary thinking that motivates employees and leads to superior long-term performance.[1]

- *Establishing short- and long-term goals of the firm.* Goals translate the firm's mission and vision into quantifiable, measurable targets. They include both strategic goals such as achieving higher market share, revenue, and asset growth and financial goals such as improving profitability, operating margins, return on assets, and return on invested capital.

- *Formulating long-term strategy.* Strategy represents the course of action taken by executives to achieve the firm's short- and long-term goals.[2] There should be a strong link between the firm's mission, vision, goals, and strategy. Mission defines the firm's business, customers, and competencies. Vision defines the firm's strategic direction. Goals translate the firm's mission and vision into measurable targets. Strategy focuses on achieving the firm's goals. In sum, strategy articulates how the firm will deliver the goals and objectives implied by the firm's mission and vision.[3]

- *Overseeing strategy execution.* The best-formulated strategies are irrelevant in the absence of good execution. Strategy formulation is often viewed as a top-down exercise because it is the firm's executives who make decisions about the firm's long-term strategic direction. In contrast, strategy implementation is often viewed as a bottom-up exercise because it is the firm's employees who implement strategy. It is, however, the firm's top management team that delegates decision-making rights to managers and employees below it. Likewise, the top management team plays a major role in motivating the firm's employee base and driving improvements in productivity.

- *Monitoring and evaluating corporate performance.* Assessing performance is more than a simple exercise of comparing actual with forecasted performance on a standardized set of accounting and stock market measures. Jim Cramer, host of the daily stock market show *Mad Money*, is fond of reminding viewers that every industry has a unique performance metric that competitors use to assess their performance relative to competitors. In the fast-food industry, for example, this metric is "same store sales." Industry competitors such as McDonald's could easily grow sales by simply building new restaurants. However, new restaurants potentially cannibalize sales from existing restaurants. Growing corporate sales at the expense of individual franchise sales would quickly alienate a company's franchise base. Therefore, great effort is made to formulate and execute strategies that build sales at the individual restaurant level. In addition to industry metrics, the most successful companies build their strategies around achieving excellence in strategic metrics. Walgreens, for example, is known for focusing on maximizing profits per store visit. A focus on this metric has the effect of focusing Walgreens on achieving the proper merchandise mix by selling a combination of goods (e.g., soft drinks and snack foods) that deliver high profit margins. Customers are willing to pay premiums for these products in return for the convenience of having a Walgreens strategically located near their home or workplace.

Composition of the Top Management Team

Each year, *Standard & Poor's Register of Corporations, Directors and Executives* [4] publishes data on more than 75,000 corporations and biographical sketches on close to 400,000 executives. A casual review of companies included in this reference source reveals a wide variation in both the number of executives and composition of job titles making up the top management teams of different companies. Each set of executives includes those with strategy-making responsibilities in the firm. Top management teams typically include most of the following job titles:

- Chairman of the board
- Chief executive officer (CEO)
- Chief operating officer (COO)
- President
- Executive vice president
- Senior vice president
- Vice president
- Chief financial officer
- Controller
- Secretary

Top Management Team Turnover Following a Merger or Acquisition

How many of your top executives do you expect will still be in your firm next year? In 2 years? In 5 years? Studies indicate that firms lose an average of 8% to 10% of their top executives each year through normal attrition. This attrition includes retirement and departures to take advantage of an offer from another firm.

Following acquisition, however, you can expect the situation to be dramatically different. In the first year following acquisition, a target firm can expect to lose about 24% of its top executives—a turnover rate about three times higher than normal. In the second year, it can expect to lose an additional 15%. That's a loss of approximately 40% of the company's original top management team in the first 2 years after the acquisition!

Table 1.1 summarizes the results of existing studies that have documented top management turnover rates in target companies following an acquisition. A graphical view of these data is shown in Figure 1.1. Jim Walsh[5] was the first to empirically analyze executive turnover rates following a merger or acquisition. Although his study sample is small, studies that followed his initial effort have found similar results. He randomly sampled 50 target companies from the Federal Trade Commission's (FTC)

Table 1.1. *Cumulative Target Company Top Management Rates Following Acquisition*

Study	Firms	Period	Portion of incumbent top management team <----- gone by end of year following acquisition ----->									
			1	2	3	4	5	6	7	8	9	10
Walsh (1988)												
Acquired firms	50	1975–1979	25.0	37.0	46.0	52.0	59.0					
Nonacquired firms	30	1975–1979	2.0	13.0	21.0	31.0	33.0					
Walsh (1989)	102	1975–1979	26.1	38.6	48.9	54.9	61.1					
Walsh & Ellwood (1991)												
Acquired firms	102	1975–1979	26.1	38.6	48.9	54.9	61.1					
Nonacquired firms	75	1975–1979	7.1	15.0	24.3	29.2	33.5					
Hambrick & Cannella (1993)	97	1980–1984	27.0	45.0	55.0	67.0						
Krishnan et al. (1997)	147	1986–1988			47.0							
Krug & Hegarty (1997)												
Acquired firms	270	1986–1988	21.2	40.5	59.9	68.4	74.8					
Nonacquired firms	120		8.1	16.3	23.6	31.6	36.9					
Krug & Nigh (1998)	101	1986–1988	20.3	39.8	61.5	69.5	77.6	82.4				
Lubatkin et al. (1999)	69	1985–1987	20.0	33.0	42.0	52.0						
Krug (2003a, 2003b)												
Acquired firms	373	1980–2004	24.7	42.4	56.5	67.0	72.8	78.6	82.2	85.4	87.1	
Nonacquired firms	100		8.4	16.7	23.8	32.2	37.2	43.1	51.8	56.3	59.9	
Krug (2008)												
Acquired firms	874	1980–2004	48.0	60.9	67.0	72.3	74.0	79.0	83.2	86.2	88.7	90.7
Nonacquired firms	145		8.5	19.1	27.7	35.4	41.8	47.3	53.4	56.4	59.7	62.8
Krug (2009)												
Acquired firms	585	1980–2004	24.0	41.9	56.0	66.3	72.8	78.3	82.0	84.7	86.3	87.8
Nonacquired firms	145		8.5	19.1	27.7	35.4	41.8	47.3	53.4	56.4	59.7	62.8
Average Turnover (Acquired Firms)			23.7	40.1	52.9	62.7	70.1	79.4	82.1	85.1	86.8	87.8
Average Turnover (Nonacquired Firms)			6.8	16.0	24.1	31.9	36.5	45.2	52.6	56.3	59.8	62.8

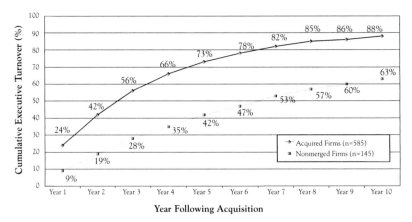

Figure 1.1. *Target company top management turnover rates following an acquisition*

Note: Cumulative turnover = Number of executives in original top management team who have departed by end of year divided by number of executives in original top management team.
Source: Jeffrey A. Krug.

Statistical Report on Mergers and Acquisitions, which reports acquisitions of U.S. manufacturing and mining firms acquired by publicly traded U.S. firms between 1975 and 1979. He collected turnover data using surveys sent to each parent company. Each company was asked to report the departure date of each target company executive who was employed at the time of the acquisition.

Based on survey responses, Walsh calculated cumulative top management turnover rates for each company in each of the 5 years following the target company's acquisition. He did not consider executives hired after the acquisition because his objective was to understand whether acquisitions lead to higher than normal turnover in the target firm's incumbent top management team—those executives in place at the time of the acquisition. He found that an average of 25% of the target company's incumbent top management team departed in the first year after the acquisition. By the fifth year, 59% of the original top management team had departed.

To determine whether these turnover rates were "higher than normal," Walsh randomly sampled 30 companies that had not been acquired during a 5-year period from *Standard & Poor's Stock Guide.*[6] Based on information reported in each company's 10-K report, he calculated top management turnover rates for each of these firms in each of 5 consecutive years of the study. Only 2% of the executives in the control group of nonmerged firms had departed by the end of the first year of the firm's initial observation. By the end of the fifth year, 33% had departed.

Structure of the Book

This book is structured around two themes. First, it examines the role that mergers and acquisitions (M&As) play in formulating and executing corporate strategy. Chapter 2 discusses global M&A trends and the different strategies that firms use to grow revenues and assets over the long term. It then discusses why M&As are a popular strategy for growing the firm over the long term and why technology and globalization trends should spur increased worldwide M&A activity over the next several decades. Chapter 3 examines the role of top management teams in formulating and executing corporate strategy. It discusses why executives matter, how top management teams are created, and the importance of managerial discretion in creating effective executive teams. Chapter 4 discusses the economic rationale for M&As and whether they create value for shareholders. Chapter 5 discusses why M&As fail. In particular, it discusses the tendency of acquiring firms to overpay, synergy creation in M&As, and the importance of industry structure in determining firm profitability and merger success.

Chapter 5 also examines the effects of M&As on target company executive teams, how acquiring firms can minimize the negative effects of an acquisition on target company leadership, and how firms can build more effective top management teams during the postmerger integration process. Chapter 6 discusses the relationship between postmerger executive turnover and postmerger performance. Current evidence suggests that turnover is a major cause of poor performance. I take a contrary view and explain why turnover can sometimes be a beneficial outcome of an acquisition. Chapter 7 discusses merger motivations, executive perceptions of different merger motives, and the strategic drivers of M&As. Chapter 8 discusses why executives stay or leave after an acquisition. Lastly, chapter 9 provides executives and acquiring firms with strategies for managing executive turnover and building more effective top management teams following a merger or acquisition.

Understanding Leadership Issues in Mergers and Acquisitions

Walsh's analysis demonstrated that executive turnover rates in acquired firms are significantly higher than comparable turnover rates in non-merged firms—in each of 5 years following an acquisition. His results offered the first empirical evidence that M&As create conditions within target companies that cause an abnormally high number of executives to depart. He also found that more senior executives (those holding the job title of chairman, CEO, or president) leave more quickly—on average within 17 months after the acquisition—than less senior executives (those holding the job title of vice president, controller, secretary, and treasurer, among others), who leave on average within 23 months.

Walsh[7] and Walsh and Ellwood[8] supplemented Walsh's[9] original study. They found that most acquiring firms take action to restructure the target company's top management team within the first 2 years after the acquisition. Target company top management turnover rates are greatest within this short period after the merger. However, the effects of this early turnover often linger for several years, as turnover rates continue to be higher than normal for a minimum of 5 years after the acquisition. They also found that turnover in the first year after the acquisition is negatively correlated with turnover in the second year. In contrast, turnover in the second year is negatively correlated with turnover in the third year. This finding suggests that parent companies have the tendency to initiate major change in a single year and do not make major subsequent changes in the target's executive team. As I argue later, the tendency of acquirers to make structural changes in the target company's top management team shortly after the acquisition and then ignore the lingering negative effects of these changes may contribute to the merger's failure.

A number of subsequent studies using similar methodologies have found similar results. For example, Hambrick and Cannella[10] analyzed 97 of the largest publicly traded U.S. companies acquired between 1980 and 1985. They calculated turnover rates for executives who held the job title of vice president or above or who were inside directors. They found that

49% of the target firms' executives departed by the end of the second year following the acquisition. In addition, they found that more senior executives (chairman, vice chairman, president, CEO, and COO) departed more quickly than less senior executives (vice presidents).

Krishnan, Miller, and Judge[11] analyzed 147 publicly traded targets acquired between 1986 and 1988. They calculated turnover rates for target company executives who held the title of senior vice president or above. By the end of the third year after the acquisition, 47% of the target company executives had departed.

Lubatkin, Schweiger, and Weber[12] analyzed 146 related acquisitions (i.e., merging companies competing in the same industry category) between 1985 and 1987. They calculated turnover rates for those target company executives who held the job title of senior vice president or above. By the end of the fourth year after the acquisition, 52% of the target executives had departed.

Several conclusions can be drawn from these early studies:

1. Mergers and acquisitions create conditions that lead to abnormally high turnover within a target company's top management team— turnover that continues to be higher than normal for at least 5 years after the acquisition.
2. The most significant turnover occurs in the first 2 years after the acquisition. About 40% of the incumbent top management team leaves within this period.
3. Acquirers are most likely to initiate major change in a single year— in most cases within the first 2 years after the acquisition. It is in this period that most involuntary turnover occurs.
4. The effect of early turnover lingers for several years. Later turnover appears to be the voluntary departure of executives, many of whom the acquirer had hoped to keep.

Although early studies provided good initial insight into the effects of acquisitions, they had a number of limitations:

1. They analyzed small samples of target companies acquired within short time frames in the 1970s and 1980s. Given the high level of M&A activity since the 1980s, a natural question is whether the

turnover effects found in M&As completed during these earlier periods also held for M&As completed during the 1990s and 2000s.

2. They focused on large, public targets. This made data collection more feasible, since data are generally not available for nonpublicly traded companies. However, a focus on public targets excludes the majority of companies involved in M&As. Only one third of M&As involve public companies. The balance—two thirds of all M&As—involves privately held targets or subsidiaries or divisions of other firms.

3. They did not examine turnover patterns across different industries. In general, the small sample sizes of early studies precluded more fine-grained analyses, including the analysis of turnover effects across different industry groups.

New Insights on Top Management Turnover Following Mergers and Acquisitions

In the 1990s, I began to document turnover rates in target company top management teams. As new research questions arose, I collected more extensive data. In the last 20 years, I have analyzed more than 10,000 M&As. To calculate executive turnover rates, I identified each target company's top management team listing in *Standard & Poor's Register of Corporations, Directors and Executives*. I then followed the company's listing in this source for the next 16 years. Only a small portion of firms survive such a long time. Most firms are merged, acquired, divested, or spun off. A large portion of all firms, especially small businesses, fail within a few years of start-up. As a result, it is likely that the turnover rates I was able to document in my research significantly underestimate the turnover rates experienced by firms in the general population. In cases of bankruptcy, for example, job losses affect a company's entire employee base, including its top management team.

My research has produced a database of 1,020 firms with top management team data over a 17-year period surrounding the firm's acquisition—beginning 6 years prior through 10 years following the target's acquisition. To build this database, I have followed the careers of more than 23,000 target company executives for 17 or more consecutive years. The size of this database permits a range of detailed analyses that heretofore have not been possible.

The Effect of Mergers and Acquisitions Over Time

To determine whether the effects found in early studies of M&As in the 1970s and 1980s held for more recent M&As, I divided my database into acquisitions completed during the 1980s, 1990s, and 2000s. Of the 1,020 firms in the database, 290 targets were acquired 2 or more times. To eliminate the effect of multiple acquisitions, I eliminated these firms from this analysis. This was a conservative approach given that turnover rates are generally significantly higher in firms acquired multiple times. However, my primary interest was in understanding the effect of single acquisitions on acquired top management teams. Therefore, I analyzed top management turnover patterns in 730 firms—585 acquired firms and a control group of 145 firms not acquired during the research period.

Figure 1.2 shows cumulative top management team turnover rates in the target companies in each of the last 3 decades. My objective was to analyze turnover rates for a minimum of 5 years after the acquisition. That meant that I could only include acquisitions completed in 2004 or earlier. This restriction limited the number of acquisitions from the 2000s, but the resulting sample was still large enough to facilitate statistical testing.

The difference in turnover patterns is evident. Tests of analysis of the variance (ANOVA) reveal that early turnover rates in companies acquired

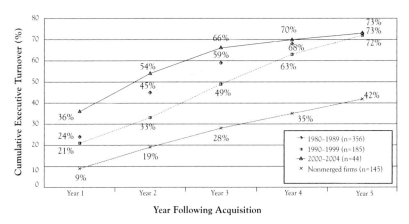

Figure 1.2. Target company top management turnover rates by year of acquisition

in the 2000s were significantly higher than in companies acquired in either the 1980s or 1990s. In the first year after the acquisition, companies acquired in the 2000s lost an average of 36% of their original top management teams. This figure compares with 24% and 21% in companies acquired in the 1980s and 1990s, respectively. By the end of the second year, companies acquired in the 2000s had lost an average of 56% of their original top management teams. Turnover rates in companies acquired during the 1980s were higher than companies acquired in the 1990s, in both the second (45% vs. 33%) and third years (59% vs. 49%) following the acquisition. By the fifth year after the acquisition, all target firms had lost a similar portion of their original top management teams—an average of 73.5% of their original top executives.

In sum, the findings of early studies—that acquisitions lead to high levels of departures among target company executives shortly after the acquisition—appears to be a common outcome of all M&As rather than a phenomenon specific to the 1970s and 1980s. Moreover, my data suggest that acquirers have become more aggressive about integrating target companies more quickly—and they appear to be more willing to replace target company executives more quickly than acquirers in the 1980s and 1990s. The effect of acquisitions in displacing target company executives appears to be getting stronger over time. This effect may partially be the result of globalization and technology trends. Data collection, communications, and travel are far easier than they were 20 years ago. Therefore, premerger analysis of acquisition candidates and postmerger integration can perhaps be undertaken more quickly than in the past.

Premerger Ownership Structure of the Target Firm

To analyze the effects of premerger ownership structure of the target firm, the database was split into three groups: (a) publicly traded targets, (b) privately held targets, and (c) subsidiaries or divisions of the selling firm. Random samples of acquisitions from the SDC Platinum database[13] show that acquisitions are generally split equally among these three target ownership groups.

Figure 1.3 shows the cumulative top management turnover rates for each of these groups. Analysis of the variance showed no significant

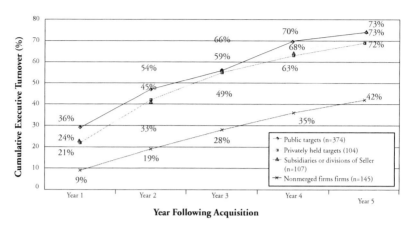

Figure 1.3. Target company top management turnover rates by premerger ownership structure

differences among these three acquisition types. This fact may surprise many. Unlike publicly traded firms, privately held companies cannot be acquired without their consent. Therefore, executives in privately held firms are in a better position to negotiate favorable terms that guarantee their continued employment after the acquisition. Anecdotal evidence suggests, however, that many privately held companies are sold by their owners as they near retirement. In these cases, the departure of target executives shortly after the acquisition represents a desirable outcome for business owners.

Although some business owners retire shortly after the acquisition, my interviews with many small business owners indicate that many stay on after the acquisition. A large number, however, become discontent with how their company is run by the new owners. Others become discontent with their loss of autonomy and having to report to a corporate parent. As a result, many executives depart in the second or third year after the acquisition.

Of the three ownership groups, subsidiary or divisional targets experience the greatest level of executive turnover—29%—in the first year after the acquisition. After the first year, however, the level and pattern of turnover are similar to those in the public and privately held targets. A large portion of the high early turnover in subsidiary or divisional targets represents executives who rotated into the subsidiary or division on short-term assignments. Following the acquisition, they choose to return to the parent company. Indeed, many large, diversified companies frequently rotate their executives through their divisions on short-term assignments as a means of transferring parent company capabilities and training future executives.

These results show that different premerger ownership structures of the target firm may affect the reasons why executives depart at high levels following the acquisition. However, these results also provide strong evidence that acquisitions in general—regardless of premerger ownership structure—create conditions that lead to higher turnover than normal among the target company's executives shortly after the acquisition.

Executive Turnover Differences by Industry

Table 1.2 breaks cumulative top management turnover rates into six industry groups: (a) financial services (banks, insurance companies, and securities firms); (b) telecommunications; (c) oil and gas; (d) consumer goods; (e) retail; (f) manufacturing; and (g) service. The data show stark differences in turnover patterns by industry. Turnover is lowest in the retail and telecommunications industries shortly after the acquisition; it is highest in financial services and consumer goods. Over time, these patterns change. In the long run, turnover in financial services is significantly lower than in all other industry categories, despite its high level of turnover immediately after the acquisition. Turnover is highest in the oil and gas and retail industries over the long term. In both of the latter industries, 93% of the original top management teams of the target firms are gone by the end of the fifth year after the acquisition.

One possible explanation for the high turnover rates in these industries may be the intensity of reporting that both industries receive in the new media. The price of oil and growth in retail sales are both reported on a regular basis. Reports are often followed by strong negative reactions and intense political debate when oil prices—and oil company profits—rise. Lower-than-expected retail sales, especially during holiday seasons, are highly reported, can affect consumer satisfaction indices, and frequently generate political debate over economic policy. Events

Table 1.2. *Cumulative Target Company Top Management Turnover Rates (%) by Industry—Year 1 Through 10 Following the Acquisition*

Industry	Firms	1	2	3	4	5	6	7	8	9	10
Financial services	67	27%	43%	52%	62%	68%	70%	75%	78%	78%	79%
Telecom	40	21%	43%	62%	67%	72%	78%	81%	81%	82%	83%
Oil & gas	51	23%	42%	62%	76%	83%	88%	90%	91%	92%	93%
Consumer	129	29%	42%	55%	66%	74%	80%	81%	85%	87%	88%
Retail	101	22%	40%	58%	69%	76%	82%	87%	90%	92%	93%
Manufacturing	152	22%	44%	57%	65%	71%	76%	81%	84%	86%	87%
Retail	45	21%	36%	46%	60%	66%	76%	80%	4%	5%	91%
Merged firms	585	24%	42%	56%	6%	73%	78%	2%	85%	86%	88%
Nonmerged firms	145	9%	19%	28%	35%	42%	47%	53%	56%	60%	63%

surrounding oil and retail are relatively more transparent, more highly publicized, and more easily understood by the general public. Constant public scrutiny may motivate more constant change in these industries. This would explain why target companies in these industries have relatively lower short-term but higher long-term executive turnover rates after an acquisition. Cumulative structural changes in these firms have a cumulative effect that takes time before they become apparent.

These findings suggest that different industry structures may require different integration approaches. Executives, like other resources, may be viewed as more or less important depending on the structural characteristics and evolving structure of the firm's industry. Therefore, the structural characteristics of the firm's industry, driving forces that are changing the focus of profitability in the firm's industry, and the firm's position in the product life cycle—whether start-up, high growth, mature, or declining—all change the nature of the integration process. These characteristics also influence the desirability of retaining target company executives after an acquisition. These industry effects are discussed in greater detail in chapter 8.

Mergers and acquisitions continue to be an important corporate strategy for growing the firm over the long term. A large portion of academic studies have concluded that a majority—more than half—fail or fail to live up to expectations despite their popularity. The evidence is clear that M&As have a profound effect on target company top management teams. A large portion of an acquired company's executives will depart within a few years following the acquisition. The departure of key target executives, however, is an important reason why many mergers fail. Acquirers that proactively manage the merger process in ways that lead to the retention of key target company executives and quickly reestablish leadership stability in the target's executive ranks have a greater chance of merger success.

CHAPTER 2

Mergers and Acquisitions

I can only describe the entire merging process as being full of secrets, lies, tricks, and games with little or no consideration for the very excellent management team that made this a valuable business.

They did not explore synergies or mutual growth but went straight for dominance and control. They pretty much left it up to empire-building subsidiary managers less qualified than our own managers to manage the business.

We have since become politicized and bureaucratic and been sucked into their big corporate culture. Our new managers have indulged in excessive and unwise capital spending. They have made acquisitions for the sake of growth that were not strategically wise. We have lost direction and focus.

Their actions have led to lower margins and the lost attractiveness of our businesses.

—Former chairman of the board reflecting on the acquisition of his firm by a conglomerate several years before (1 year after the acquisition, he "retired")

Global Merger and Acquisition Activity

All firms must grow to survive over time. Overwhelmingly, firms prefer mergers and acquisitions (M&As) over other strategies such as internal development, joint ventures, or strategic alliances as their primary strategy for meeting long-term goals, achieving growth objectives, and improving the firm's competitive position (see Figure 2.1). The popularity of M&As is evident by the sheer number of transactions completed each year. According to Thomson Reuters, more than 43,000 M&As valued at $4.2 trillion were completed in 2007—an all-time high.[1] The current crisis in world financial markets took a toll on global M&A activity in 2008 as global M&A volume fell to 38,000 transactions valued at $2.9 trillion—a 31% drop from the previous year (see Figure 2.2).

Strategies for Long-Term Growth of the Firm

Despite the negative effects of the current banking crisis, globalization and technology trends indicate that M&As will continue to be a primary

Corporate growth strategies
- Internal development
- Mergers and acquisitions
- Joint ventures
- Strategic alliances

Business growth strategies
- Horizontal integration
- Geographic expansion
- Vertical integration
- Diversification

Figure 2.1. Growth strategies

driver of worldwide economic activity. They will also continue to play a major role in shaping firms' long-term corporate strategies. Firms expand using a variety of strategies, but four strategies are most common:

1. *Horizontal integration.* The most common strategy, especially for firms in an early stage of development, is to pursue growth in sales and market share for their existing products and services in their existing geographic market. An example of this tendency is Bank of America's acquisition of Security Pacific Bank in 1992, which increased Bank of America's leadership position in financial services in California.

2. *Geographic expansion (market extension).* When markets mature, firms typically respond by expanding existing products and services

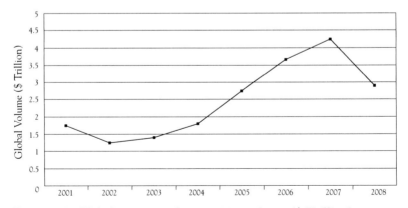

Figure 2.2. Global merger and acquisition volume ($ Trillion)

into other geographic markets. Deutsche Bank's acquisition of Bankers Trust in 1999, for example, allowed Deutsche Bank to solidify its position in commercial banking in the United States.

3. *Vertical integration.* A firm's profitability can be affected by important suppliers that demand higher prices and by powerful distributors that demand lower purchase prices. In addition, unmotivated distributors can put a cap on sales growth and create negative perceptions among consumers. Firms can reduce supplier power by acquiring them. Alternatively, they can integrate backward by creating their own internal capabilities for sourcing raw materials. Firms can reduce distributor power by acquiring them or by creating internal distribution networks that are controlled and operated by the firm's own personnel. Integrating distribution channels into the firm's value chain not only gives firms greater control over distribution activities but can be a means of acquiring new sales outlets. PepsiCo, for example, acquired Kentucky Fried Chicken in 1986, which created a new outlet for Pepsi-Cola products.

4. *Diversification.* Firms are constantly looking for ways of leveraging their existing resources and capabilities in new businesses, especially when existing businesses mature. An example is Procter & Gamble's acquisition of Iams, a leading manufacturer of pet foods, in 1999. Iams added to P&G's portfolio of 44 consumer brands that today contribute more than $500 million to P&G's annual revenues.[2]

M&As as a Long-Term Corporate Growth Strategy

Acquisitions Versus Internal Development

When and under what circumstances are acquisitions a preferred strategy for entering new businesses and markets compared to other strategy modes such as internal development, joint venture, or strategic alliance? How do firms make choices among them?[3]

The choice between acquisition and internal development (i.e., greenfield investment) is strongly influenced by the firm's resources and capabilities (see Figure 2.3). Internal development takes time—on average, it takes 8 or more years to bring a new product, service, or technology to market.[4] Resource-based theory provides a basis for understanding why some firms are able to enter new businesses successfully and sustain profitability over the long term, when competitors cannot. Long-term competitive advantage depends on the firm's ability to create products, services, and technologies that are difficult to imitate. In theoretical terms, the most successful firms create unique sets of resources and organizational capabilities that are rare, valuable, imperfectly imitable, and nonsubstitutable.[5] Consequently, firms with unique and intangible competencies are in the strongest position to internally develop and successfully commercialize new products, services, and technologies.

Consider Honda, which began as a manufacturer of small clip-on motors to propel bicycles. Honda's early leadership in small engine design led to motorcycle production that is presently unrivaled—it sold more than 9.3 million motorcycles worldwide in 2008.[6] Honda's product portfolio today covers a wide range of both street (touring, cruisers, choppers, sport, motard, dual sport, and scooters) and off-road (trail, motocross, and ATV) motorcycles. Honda has leveraged its capabilities in small engine manufacturing and design by diversifying into a wide range of motorized products such as automobiles, outboard motors, personal watercraft, boat engines, snow blowers, lawn mowers, tillers, trimmers, generators, pumps, and power units for home heat and air conditioning. In sum, firms that successfully establish leadership positions based on intangible assets and capabilities are in the best position to leverage capabilities in new start-up businesses.[7]

Other examples of firms with unique sets of intangible resources and capabilities include Apple and Microsoft (technological know-how); Intel and Texas Instruments (capacity to innovate ahead of competitors); and Toyota, Caterpillar, and the Walt Disney Company (imbedded cultural systems that lead to superior quality, productivity, and innovation). These intangible resources and capabilities are difficult for competitors to imitate.

In contrast, tangible resources such as raw materials, physical plants and equipment, and financial resources are rarely a basis for creating sustainable, long-term competitive advantage because advantages can be copied by competitors. Therefore, competitive advantages based on tangible assets are normally short-lived. When firms don't possess unique sets of resources and capabilities, acquisition is often the best strategy for gaining entry into new businesses. Firms can acquire them.

Competitive advantages based on patents and copyrights are also rarely a source of long-term competitive advantage. Once a patent or copyright expires, it becomes public property that can be copied and sold by competitors. Pharmaceutical companies have recently engaged in acquisitions as a means of acquiring new biologic innovations to replace their own expiring patents. Pfizer, for example, acquired Wyeth for $68 billion in January 2009, largely to acquire Wyeth's portfolio of prescription drugs such as Effexor (antidepression) and Premarin (estrogen replacement).[8] Pfizer was under increasing pressure to find replacements for its primary prescription drugs—Viagra (erectile dysfunction) and Celebrex (anti-inflammation)—which account for a major portion of Pfizer's annual sales and will expire in a few years. Other pharmaceutical companies have recently engaged in acquisitions both to replace expiring patents and to diversify into other pharmaceutical areas such as biotechnology, thereby reducing their dependence on new pharmaceutical applications. Notable examples include Roche's offer to acquire Genentech and Merck & Co.'s bid for Schering-Plough.[9]

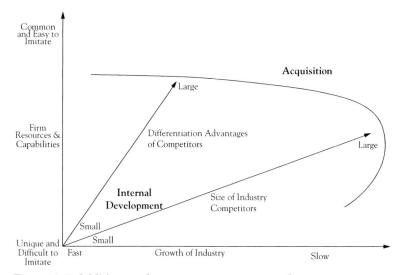

Figure 2.3. M&As as a long-term corporate growth strategy: Acquisition versus internal development

The Importance of Industry Structure

Even when firms possess unique sets of resources, capabilities, and competencies, acquisitions may still be the best strategy for entering new businesses. The structure of a firm's industry has a strong influence over the firm's decision to use acquisition or internal development to enter new businesses. Internally developing new products and technologies can be an effective strategy in fast-growing markets that can absorb additional capacity. In mature or declining markets, however, internally developing new products is undesirable because it adds capacity to the industry when capacity already exceeds demand. Acquisitions are a more effective strategy in mature or slower-growing markets because they involve the acquisition of existing market share without adding capacity to the industry.

Even in fast-growing markets, however, internal development still may not be an effective strategy for market entry when barriers to entry are high. The structure of the firm's industry determines the intensity of competition and influences firm profitability. As Michael Porter from Harvard Business School commented, "The essence of formulating competitive strategy is relating a company to its environment."[10] Firms increase profitability by establishing strong competitive positions in their industry that are difficult for competitors to overcome. The study of industry structure and its effect on firm profitability is grounded in industrial organization economics (sometimes referred to as the I/O theory of strategic management). When an industry is composed of firms selling homogeneous products, profitability is determined by size.[11] Large firms have greater scale and scope efficiencies. New entrants are deterred from entering the industry because they cannot match the cost advantages of the industry's existing competitors.[12] New entrants, therefore, may only be able to overcome these disadvantages through acquisition of an existing competitor.

Other industries are composed of competitors with strong differentiation advantages. Differentiation may exist in brand (e.g., Procter & Gamble, Unilever, and Nestlé) or in technology (e.g., Boeing, Siemens, and Hitachi). Successful differentiation among an industry's competitors forces new entrants to make substantial investments in advertising (to overcome brand disadvantages) or in research and development (R&D) (to overcome disadvantages in technology and innovation). For example, an industry such as semiconductors requires high capital costs to establish production and develop new technologies. Semiconductor wafer facilities currently cost an average of $3 billion to construct.[13] As a result, firms like Texas Instruments and Intel sell their products globally to increase volume. Higher volume is critical for covering high R&D, product development, and production costs.

Large-scale production is also critical for developing scale and scope efficiencies. These efficiencies become increasingly critical as technologies mature, which shifts industry competition from premium-priced differentiation strategies to standardized, low-cost strategies. The nature of the semiconductor market, therefore, makes it extremely difficult for new entrants. Even if a new competitor is able to raise enough capital to begin production, it must quickly generate enough global revenue to offset the low-cost positions of existing competitors. Consequently, the existence of high entry barriers in an industry makes acquisitions of established competitors the only feasible strategy for entry.

In sum, acquisitions have a variety of advantages over other strategy modes. The most notable include the following (see Figure 2.4):

1. *Speed of market entry.* It takes several years to bring most new products or technologies to market, and a high percentage of new businesses fail within a few years. Acquisitions enable acquirers to acquire ongoing, established businesses.

2. *Cost.* The cost of developing a new business organization to produce and distribute new products, services, and technologies internally often far outweighs the cost of acquiring an existing business.

3. *Risk.* Acquiring a business with an established position in its industry is often a significantly less risky strategy for entering new businesses than introducing new, untried products to the marketplace.

4. *Financing and deal structure.* Firms often don't have sufficient cash or debt financing capacity to support the development of a new business internally. In the case of acquisitions, firms can acquire ongoing businesses using stock in addition to cash and debt financing. Therefore, acquisitions give firms the opportunity to expand into new businesses when internal development isn't feasible. The use of stock to finance acquisitions can, however, be a risky strategy

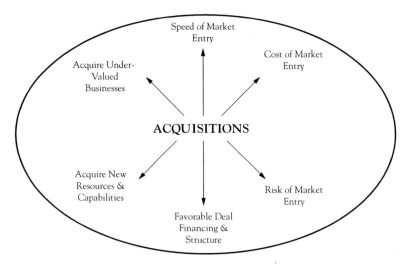

Figure 2.4. Acquisitions versus internal development: The advantages of acquisitions

because it can dilute the stock value of existing shareholders. For example, Pfizer, the world's largest pharmaceutical company, under the leadership of Henry McKinnell, engaged in an acquisition spree financed primarily using stock-for-stock transactions. Between 1999 and 2006, Pfizer's stock price fell from $50 to $30 per share—an estimated loss in shareholder stock value of about $140 billion![14]

5. *Developing new resources and capabilities.* Firms may not have adequate resources and capabilities to successfully launch a new business. Acquisitions are a means of acquiring resources and capabilities and then learning them.

6. *Acquiring undervalued businesses.* Acquisitions are a means for acquiring firms to benefit by buying undervalued companies that are managed by ineffective management. By replacing incompetent managers with their own managers, acquirers can improve target performance and either continue to operate the target or sell it at a profit.

In some cases, firms choose to engage in joint ventures and strategic alliances as a means of entering new businesses.[15] These modes of entry offer a range of benefits for firms to develop and commercialize new products, services, and technologies:

1. They are a means of jointly sharing both the risk and cost of developing new products, services, and technologies.
2. They are a means of developing new businesses using shared resources and technologies.
3. They are a means of gaining access to a partner's distribution channels and marketing resources.
4. They allow firms to enter foreign markets at less risk and cost. Partnering with a local firm is often less costly and risky because the local firm has greater knowledge and experience operating in its own market.
5. They lower political risk when operating in foreign markets. Foreign governments are much less likely to regulate or expropriate the assets of foreign firms when the firm's operations are jointly owned and operated by a local firm.

Joint ventures and strategic alliances, however, are often difficult to implement. In particular, partners may resist sharing proprietary resources and secrets out of fear that the other may appropriate them. In many cases, joint ventures and alliances are terminated when a partner concludes that ongoing costs of the relationship outweigh benefits. Thus, the most important disadvantage of these alternative strategy modes of entry is that they require that firms share their resources and capabilities with other firms. Doing so makes it more difficult for firms to protect internal competencies that lead to long-term sustainable competitive advantage. It is not surprising, then, that in more than two-thirds of the cases, firms choose to expand using M&As.

Globalization and Technology Trends

Following World War II, few international firms existed outside the United States, as Japan and Europe focused on rebuilding their domestic economies. Most countries erected high import tariffs and other trade barriers to protect domestic companies from outside competition. As a result, most international firms were forced to establish local production in foreign markets as a means of circumventing trade barriers. Because competition was localized and technological changes were slow to evolve, most firms preferred to develop new products and services internally.

The world has changed dramatically during the last 30 years. Tariffs and other trade barriers have been significantly reduced or eliminated as a result of the General Agreement on Tariffs and Trade (GATT). Between 1947 and 1997, GATT successfully negotiated reductions in tariffs and restrictions on capital flows worldwide. GATT was replaced by the World Trade Organization (WTO) in 1995. Although its work is far from done, the WTO continues to negotiate and implement new trade agreements among member countries. The reduction of tariffs and other restrictions on capital flows has allowed international firms to more easily shift assets across national boundaries to take advantage of differences in wage, capital, and asset costs. The effect has been to encourage cross-border investment and, in turn, greater M&A activity.

The rapid evolution of technology in computers, semiconductors, telecommunications, pharmaceuticals, and chemicals, among other industries, has also promoted globalization. As R&D and product development costs have risen, and product life cycles have shortened, firms have come under greater pressure to increase sales volumes to cover higher fixed costs. Firms have responded by selling their products and services globally to cover escalating R&D and product development costs. By shifting assets worldwide to take advance of lower wage and capital costs and standardizing products and services, firms can simultaneously increase sales, lower costs, and improve operating margins.

The Multinational Enterprise (MNE)

Firms based in the United States and Europe each account for about 40% of global M&A volume.[16] The effect of globalization and technology trends has been to encourage greater investments across national boundaries and this, in turn, has stimulated cross-border M&A activity. A rising percentage of all transactions—now close to 45%—are cross-border. Foreign investment is largely the domain of large multinational enterprises (MNEs)—firms that control productive assets outside their home country.[17] The United Nations Conference on Trade and Development (UNCTD) estimates that MNEs based in Japan, North America, and Europe control more than 85% of the world's foreign investment.[18] Moreover, cross-border acquisitions are rising while greenfield investments (i.e., internal development) have been declining. Thus, current trends show that M&As are increasingly the preferred market entry strategy for MNEs.

During the last decade, rapidly industrializing economies such as China, India, South Korea, Mexico, and Brazil have begun to develop their own transnational capabilities. Examples of this development include PetroChina (oil and gas) and China Telecom (telecommunications) in China, Samsung Electronics (semiconductors) and Hyundai Motors (automobiles) in Korea, Reliance Industries (oil and gas) and Bharti Airtel (telecommunications) in India, Cemex (construction) and Vitro (glass) in Mexico, and Petrobras Petróleo (oil and gas) and Banco do Brasil in Brazil. Although a majority of cross-border transactions involve firms based in Europe and North America, firms based in these emerging markets have made a number of significant acquisitions that have reshaped their industries. Notable examples include Lenovo's (China) acquisition of IBM's computer division in 2005 and Tata Motors's (India) acquisition of Range Rover and Jaguar in 2008.

In sum, the rising importance of international business, the popularity of acquisitions as the preferred strategy for foreign market entry, and the emergence of industrializing countries such as China, India, and Brazil, which are rapidly developing their own transnational capabilities to challenge MNEs from developing countries, indicate that M&As will continue to grow in importance over the next several decades.

CHAPTER 3

Top Management Teams

The acquiring company's post-merger strategy involved a strong effort to absorb, sublimate, and force-fit our company into their corporate mold. They significantly overpaid for our company and that led them to push excessive goals and expectations on our company to improve performance.

I promised—indeed, I owed!—my team one year for transition. Our hope for a good process, unfortunately, never came to pass. The emphasis was almost immediately on compliance and conformity. While our exceptionally strong and accomplished top management team was a major part of what was "bought," they immediately attempted to take over and run the business—which we knew better than they did!

The new owners cost themselves millions of lost profits.

—Former chief executive officer discussing how members of his top management team were treated by acquiring company executives

The Chief Executive Officer

The chief executive officer (CEO) is responsible for managing the firm as a whole—establishing its vision, creating a mission, formulating and executing strategy, constructing a corporate portfolio of businesses that create synergies and improve performance, allocating resources among competing units, and, ultimately, evaluating performance.[1]

Executives—with some notable exceptions—are rewarded when their companies prosper and take the fall when their companies falter. Books are filled with stories of executives who almost single-handedly took the reigns of their companies and made them great. There are many examples of companies known as much by their founders as by the company itself—for example, Steve Jobs at Apple, Fred Smith at Federal Express, and J. W. Marriott at Marriott International. Other companies continue to be associated with their founders or strong former chief executives, even though the chief executive has long since died, retired, or moved on—for example, Sam Walton at Wal-Mart, Jack Welch at General Electric, Ray Kroc at McDonald's, and Michael Eisner at Walt Disney. Other companies are increasingly known by rising chief executives who have helped restore strong performance to their firms after periods of weakness—for example, Jim Skinner at McDonald's and Indra Nooyi at PepsiCo.

Not all executive stories are inspiring. Jürgen Schrempp rose to become CEO at Daimler-Benz in 1995. He later orchestrated a merger with Chrysler that cost his company $37 billion in a stock-swap deal. Culture clashes and mistrust between the two companies—largely caused by Schrempp's own actions—took a toll on Chrysler's morale and productivity.[2] Schrempp was removed as CEO in 2006. In 2007, Daimler sold Chrysler to a private equity firm for $7 billion. One year later, the Bush administration provided $17 billion to Chrysler and General Motors to help them sustain ongoing operations and avoid bankruptcy.

Unethical or illegal actions taken by executives have also shaken public confidence in corporate entities and highly paid executives from time to time. An unforgettable example was the bankruptcy of Enron in 2001, which was brought about by accounting irregularities, false statements made to shareholders, and securities fraud. Jeffrey Skilling (former CEO) and Kenneth Lay (former chairman) were both later convicted on numerous counts of securities fraud. Lay died of a heart attack while vacationing in Colorado before he could be sentenced. Another widely reported example is the conviction of Dennis Kozlowski, former CEO at Tyco, on several counts of fraud and grand larceny associated with the granting of unauthorized bonuses and personal use of company funds.

In sum, a firm's CEO plays an important role in creating a long-term corporate vision, shaping and executing corporate strategy, and motivating employees. When successful, they can earn herolike status. When unsuccessful, many executives are brought down in disgrace and do much to damage the public trust. Regardless of the organizational outcome, it is widely believed that the CEO is the primary driver of a firm's long-term success or failure.

It is not surprising, then, that the most senior target company executives—in particular, the chairman and CEO (often one and the same)—are the first to be terminated following an acquisition. One of the most important roles played by the firm's CEO is symbolic. When major strategic change is initiated, such as a merger, acquisition, divestiture, reorganization, restructuring, or employee downsizing, it is the CEO who addresses employees and the news media. It is the CEO who answers to the firm's board of directors and seeks its approval for such actions and then takes responsibility for their outcomes. CEOs also play a major role in molding and publicizing the core values of the organization in ways that shape corporate culture and motivate employees.

When a firm is acquired, the company's CEO can play an important role in helping the acquiring entity to integrate the target company and transition it to the new company's systems, policies, and procedures. However, target company CEOs who resist integration or refuse to cooperate with new management can jeopardize the acquiring company's integration efforts. As a result, many acquiring companies ask the target CEO to leave shortly after the acquisition to prevent potential resistance, even though such resistance may not have been openly expressed. In other cases, acquirers may terminate the target's CEO and other senior executives for symbolic reasons—to make a strong statement to target company personnel and stockholders that they are now in charge.

Why Companies Fail

Firms fail for a variety of reasons—bad management, poor strategy, lack of competitive advantage, industry turbulence, and economic recession (see Figure 3.1). In his bestseller *Good to Great*, Jim Collins profiled 11 companies from the Fortune 500 that generated 15 consecutive years of superior stock returns—an achievement unmatched by the rest of the Fortune 500.[3] Many of the concepts introduced by Collins, including the "Level 5 Leader" and "First Who . . . Then What," are based on the assumption that leaders—and people—matter. Great companies have great leaders who hire, motivate, and retain the right people. Collins also introduces several other concepts that relate to strategy such as "Confront the Brutal Facts," "The Hedgehog Concept," and "A Culture of Discipline."

An underlying assumption of each of these concepts is that great strategy is at the heart of great companies. Great leaders hire great people, create great strategies, execute strategies effectively, and create great corporate cultures that support the company's strategy and create productive, motivated, and satisfied employees. There are many examples of great leaders who fit this profile, among them Charles Cork at Walgreens, George Cain at Abbott, Darwin Smith at Kimberly-Clark, and Alan Wurtzel at Circuit City.

- ■ **Poor management**
- ■ **Poor strategy**
  - ➤ Inability to successfully differentiate the firm's products, services, and technologies.
  - ➤ Escalating costs.

- ■ **Economic recession**
  - ➤ Industry maturity.
  - ➤ Intensity of competition.
  - ➤ Entry of new competitors.
  - ➤ Emergence of disruptive technologies.

Figure 3.1. Why companies fail

I require all of my MBA and executive MBA students to read *Good to Great*. Sometimes they respond by pointing out that companies like Circuit City have since failed. They ask, "Why should we believe the findings of Collins's research? Doesn't this just prove that this research is no longer valid?" As Table 3.1 shows, a number of the "great companies" on Collins's list have, indeed, faltered—Circuit City closed its doors in 2009 and Fannie Mae was placed in conservatorship of the Federal Housing Finance Agency (FHFA) in 2008 to save it from failure. Other companies like Kimberly-Clark, Kroger, and Walgreens have lost ground to other competitors in their industry.

In turn, I point out that all companies encounter difficulties throughout their lives because of bad management decisions, challenges from new competitors, industry maturity, government regulations, and changes in industry structure. Consider Harley-Davidson. Founded in 1903, it continued to grow in popularity for 60 years before it was acquired by American Machinery and Foundry (AMF) in 1969. AMF reduced Harley's work force and slashed research and development (R&D). The quality of Harley's product plummeted and Harley's labor force went on strike. Motorcyclists rate the AMF period as a disaster. In the 1980s, with the help of U.S. import restrictions on large Japanese motorcycles, Harley management and employees took control of the company. Copying the just-in-time inventory and quality control methods of Honda,

Table 3.1. List of Great Companies[a]

Company	Industry	Years studied	2009 Fortune Most Admired Ranking[b]
Abbott	Pharmaceuticals	1974–1989	3rd of 7 firms (4)
Circuit City	Retail	1982–1997	Bankrupt (2009)
Fannie Mae	Savings and loan	1984–1999	Placed in conservatorship of FHFA (2008)
Gillette	Cosmetics	1980–1995	Acquired by P&G (2005)
Kimberly-Clark	Cosmetics	1972–1987	5th of 5 firms (4)
Kroger	Food and drug	1973–1988	5th of 8 firms (2)
Nucor	Metals	1975–1990	8th of 8 firms (9)
Altria Group	Tobacco	1964–1979	1st of 5 firms (1)
Pitney Bowes	Office equipment	1973–1988	Not ranked
Walgreens	Food and drugstores	1975–1990	6th of 8 firms (7)
Wells Fargo	Megabanks	1983–1998	4th of 7 firms (3)

[a] *Source:* Collins (2001), p. 7.
[b] 2008 company ranking out of number of competitors rated (previous year ranking shown in parentheses).

it improved the quality of its motorcycles and focused on developing a successful niche strategy in the heavy cruiser segment.

Harley focused on building a niche strategy based on customization, design, and the unique sound of its engines—all features that met the needs of Harley's highly individualistic, patriotic, nonconformist customer base. Instead of advertising to the mass market, it focused on reinforcing loyalty among customers after the sale. It created a Harley Owners Group (HOG), which sponsors motorcycle rallies and charity events. Despite its disadvantages—Honda sold more than 9.3 million motorcycles to Harley's 313,769 in 2008—Harley has created one of the most loyal customer groups in the world.[4] It is a wonderful example of how a small company can succeed using a unique niche strategy when faced with a larger competitor with advantages at almost every stage of its value chain.

Top Management Teams

In their book *The Wisdom of Teams*, Katzenbach and Smith refer to the top management team as a "small number of people with complementary skills who are committed to a common purpose, performance goals, and approach for which they hold themselves mutually accountable."[5] A top management team's executives typically report directly to the company's CEO or general manager and have decision-making responsibilities that determine the strategic direction of the firm.[6] In most organizations, the top management team includes both functional and product heads. In global organizations, it also includes executives who manage the firm's business operations in specific regions of the world. Early theorists argued that strategy is influenced by those who are in a position to exercise power within the organization. Child referred to this group of individuals as the organization's "dominant coalition," which might include board members, shareholders, and union leaders, as well as executives who might yield power at any time.[7]

The current view in the field of strategy, however, focuses on the firm's top management team as the dominant group in shaping and influencing firm strategy, structure, and performance. It is an important group of executives at the top of the organization that shares in strategy making and takes responsibility for the firm's long-term performance. Top management—and leadership—is, therefore, a shared activity that incorporates the differing viewpoints of executives, many of whom may have very different backgrounds, experiences, and opinions.

It is rare for decision making to be controlled entirely by the CEO. This is especially the case in large organizations that manage a diversified portfolio of businesses across multiple geographic regions. In large, diversified firms, CEOs could not possibly manage the complexities of all decisions made throughout the organization, nor would they have the time. The effective management of large organizations necessarily requires that decisions be made by different managers at different levels of the organization.[8]

The use of the word "team" might also be viewed as a misnomer in that top management teams rarely operate as real teams. This view is described in detail by Jon Katzenbach in his book *Teams at the Top*.[9] Real teams work together to set common goals, collectively formulate and execute strategy, and jointly evaluate performance. In practice, top management teams rarely work together collectively, except when they come together for periodic strategic planning sessions or in times of crisis management. Instead, the typical top management team's members—the leaders of the firm's different functional, product, and geographic groups—work individually to set goals, formulate and execute strategy, and manage and coordinate the activities of the divisions under their charge. A large portion of an executive's decisions are made without the explicit approval of the CEO and often without communicating their actions to him or her directly.

The Allocation of Decision-Making Rights

Organizations provide a significant economic benefit to society in that they efficiently gather, manage, and coordinate resources in order to produce products and services of value to consumers.[10] In theoretical terms, firms are "legal fictions which serve as a nexus for a set of contracting relationships among individuals," whereby individual employees negotiate and enter into contracts with outside parties (e.g., suppliers and vendors) in the name of the firm.[11] Organizations are also a means of partitioning and allocating decision-making rights.[12] All organizations have unique organizational structures that define who does what and where. The organizational structure is a way for the firm to define the roles and responsibilities of individual executives and employees. In defining an employee's role, the firm also grants certain decision-making rights to the employee to perform those functions he or she performs the best.

In public corporations, shareholders are the owners. Most shareholders, however, have neither the time nor the knowledge to effectively manage and monitor the firm's performance. Rather, they elect a board of directors to perform these functions for them. In doing so, shareholders are allocating a portion of their decision-making rights to the firm's board. The board, however, is composed of directors—primarily executives working full-time in other firms—who only meet several times a year. Therefore, the board is not in a position to manage day-to-day operations. Instead, it names a CEO to manage the firm's day-to-day operations in its place. In doing so, the board is allocating a portion of its decision-making rights to the CEO (see Figure 3.2). In turn, the CEO

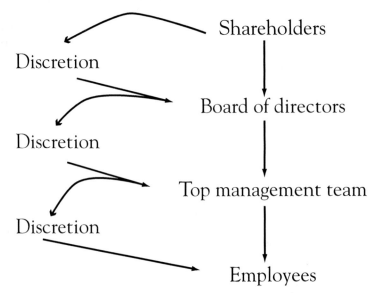

Figure 3.2. Managerial discretion: The principal–agent relationship

hires executives to serve on the firm's top management team. Each executive, in turn, hires employees to perform functions below him or her. In each case, decision-making rights are partitioned and allocated to those who can perform each activity most effectively. Thus, organizations play an important societal role in efficiently allocating resources among competing ends to improve the public welfare.

Managerial Discretion

Executives are different from other employees. Most employees have well-defined responsibilities that give them little latitude to make decisions that stray too far from the guidelines of their job. In contrast, executives typically have broadly defined responsibilities that give them wide latitude in making decisions. Relative to other employees, executives have great freedom to use their personal judgment and intuition to make decisions that affect the firm. Executives require a wide degree of latitude in making decisions because they must respond to a wide range of changes in their competitive environment—from suppliers, competitors, distributors, and other stakeholders—on a day-to-day basis. Executives must rely on their experiences and intuition to effectively interpret and respond to these competitive changes. Discretion is an important component of leadership—it gives the executive the ability to use his or her personal expertise, experience, and judgment to make decisions that lead to positive organizational outcomes.

The extent of an executive's discretion, however, is rarely known. How wide is an executive's latitude of action? How much discretion can an executive use in his or her decision making? When an executive takes actions or makes decisions that more senior executives, shareholders, or other stakeholders of the firm view as inappropriate, he or she becomes subject to reprimand. In the worst case scenario, he or she is removed.

The actions of John Thain after he was named CEO of Merrill Lynch & Co. at the end of 2007 are a good example. Thain replaced then-CEO Stan O'Neal as losses mounted from the company's declining real estate investments. After taking office, Thain reportedly spent $1.2 million to refurbish his offices at Merrill's headquarters in New York. These expenditures were widely reported in the news media. The expenditures were newsworthy for their enormity. In addition, many questioned how a CEO could spend company funds on lavish, arguably personal furnishings at a time the company was considering layoffs in response to its declining performance. Soon after, Merrill reported a net loss of $8.6 billion for the 2007 fiscal year.[13] Losses continued to mount in 2008. Thain responded by courting buyers. Bank of America stepped forward and acquired Merrill in a stock deal valued at $50 billion at the end of 2008.

Three weeks after the acquisition, Thain was terminated by Bank of America's CEO, Kenneth Lewis. Lewis was unhappy with Merrill's higher-than-expected fourth quarter loss of $15.3 billion. Merrill later reported a net loss of $27.6 billion for the 2008 fiscal year.[14] Lewis was also unhappy with Thain's handling of large bonuses to Merrill executives in December 2008.[15] Thain's actions were particularly troubling because they occurred after Bank of America had accepted $75 billion in U.S. government bailout funds to keep the bank solvent. Approximately $30 billion of this amount was used to help Bank of America acquire Merrill several months before—to prevent Merrill's bankruptcy![16]

Carl von Clausewitz, the great Prussian general, whose treatise on military strategy *Vom Kriege* (*On War*) was published in 1867, compared war to commerce, which he referred to as a conflict of human interests and activities. He further compared war to politics, which he viewed to be a kind of commerce on a larger scale.[17] He viewed strategy largely as a game of competitive positioning that depended on social interactions and a leader's ability to interpret, negotiate, and outmaneuver his or her competitors. Strategy was best viewed as a social process that resulted in interplay among players. Because people often interpret the same events differently and competitors often respond in unanticipated ways, Clausewitz viewed the outcome of direct conflict as largely unpredictable.

Strategy making in the firm is also largely unpredictable. Executives must use their judgment to respond to a wide array of events and stakeholders' positions. Discretion is a critical component of managing strategy making in the firm and is critical to the firm's success. Managing discretion, however, is a double-edged sword. On the one hand, organizations derive enormous benefit from executives who have the experience and judgment to effectively respond to ever-changing environmental conditions. On the other hand, the boundaries of an executive's actions are rarely known. Outcomes are difficult to predict. In some cases, the board, shareholders, and the public may interpret the executive's actions in ways that force his or her departure.

The Composition of Top Management Teams

Top management teams work more effectively when a high degree of trust and loyalty exists among top management team members. Trust and loyalty promote open communication and the sharing of information. Communication and information sharing promote more effective debate, which leads to better decision making.

The firm's top management team—its members and how they interact—strongly influence decision-making processes, the quality of firm strategy, and how well strategy is executed.[18] When an executive departs, important skills and capabilities of the departing individual may be lost. In addition, the departure of a valuable executive may also negatively affect top management team decision-making processes and effectiveness. The departure of key executives can break organizational inertia, disrupt leadership stability, and lead to declining performance.[19]

Poor performing firms are most likely to make changes in their executive teams.[20] Therefore, high executive turnover rates are often an indicator of financial distress. Once financially distressed, many firms continue to decline, creating a spiraling effect from which many cannot recover.[21] The selection of replacement executives is, obviously, an important strategic decision for the firm. New executives alter the structure of the existing top management team and can influence the firm's strategy, structure, internal processes, and performance.[22]

One of the most important roles that a chief executive plays is to construct an effective top management team that is both competent and loyal.[23] Mergers, acquisitions, divestitures, and corporate restructuring are important organizational events because they lead to significant changes in the composition of the top management team.

The critical question is whether executive turnover that follows acquisitions and other corporate restructurings lead to higher or lower firm performance.

CHAPTER 4

Do Mergers and Acquisitions Create Value?

The acquiring company's only motive was to milk the company of cash flow and raise their own return-on-investment. They destroyed employee, customer, and supplier morale. The merger involved a leveraged buyout and a junk bond issue was necessary to bridge the financial gap. The liberal nature with which they applied questionable accounting procedures to make financials look better before going public with the bond issue was abominable. Both the public accounting firm and the SEC must have been asleep. Anyone even remotely familiar with proper accounting procedures should have been able to see through their ruse.

I had to leave. Their actions compromised my ethics both personally and professionally. They had a total disregard for our employees and the company's long-term welfare. I considered their practices to be down-right dishonest for the personal gain of a few investors.

—Former executive describing the reasons why he decided to leave shortly after his company was acquired

The Economic Rationale of Mergers and Acquisitions

A few months ago, I appeared on CNBC's *Closing Bell* with Maria Bartiromo to discuss my research on executive turnover following mergers and acquisitions (M&As). Robert Profusek, who directs the M&A practice at Jones Day, a New York-based legal firm that advises firms on corporate governance issues, was asked to comment on one of my articles, which had recently been published in *Journal of Business Strategy*.[1] Profusek disagreed with a statement I made in the article: that a large portion of M&As fail. He asserted that many M&As are driven by synergistic motives. Therefore, executive turnover is often a necessary and desirable outcome of M&As.

Profusek did have a good point. I agreed that some mergers do indeed result in top management team redundancies such as overlapping functional management skills. In these cases, efficiencies can sometimes be achieved by eliminating redundant positions. Research on M&As, however, shows that a majority of target companies are good performers, not poorly performing firms that need to be acquired in order to rid them of incompetent management.[2] Exactly the opposite is true. Most acquiring firms are attracted to companies that have something of value—technology, marketing know-how, access to distribution channels, among many other factors—on which the acquiring company would like to get its hands.

My premise was that target company executives are often critical to the success of a newly merged organization because of their firm-specific knowledge, industry experience, and long-term relationships with firm stakeholders. Retaining key executives also ensures that ongoing strategic relationships are not disrupted or terminated. Target executives can also act as an important buffer between new management and target company employees. Acquisitions create tremendous uncertainty and stress among employees. Target company executives play an important role communicating the goals of the merger to employees in ways that minimize negative behavioral effects and losses in employee productivity.

Corporate Versus Business Strategy

Growth through acquisition is a corporate-level strategy—what Jay Bourgeois at the University of Virginia terms "domain selection."[3] Corporate strategy focuses on the multibusiness or diversified firm. It is the domain of top executives who determine the portfolio of businesses in which the firm should compete. Executives create value by managing and coordinating the value-chain activities of the firm's various businesses in ways that create synergies (i.e., enhance the individual performance of each business). Such value might be created by transferring skills and competences across businesses; centralizing overhead expenses at the corporate level; and coordinating purchasing, distribution, and marketing activities.

In contrast, business or competitive strategy focuses on the single business or division of a diversified firm. Business strategy is the domain of divisional managers who formulate and execute competitive strategies in order to create sustainable competitive advantage ("domain navigation").[4] The single business or division creates competitive advantages by establishing low-cost positions in its industry or by differentiating products and services in ways that provide unique value to customers for which customers are willing to pay a premium.

Why Do Firms Organize?

Early management writers used a transaction cost perspective to explain why firms exist. This perspective originated with Ronald Coase's 1937 treatise on "The Nature of the Firm."[5] He explained that if goods and services are produced on the open market, production occurs through a series of open exchange transactions among individuals. If markets were able to operate at low cost and in the absence of uncertainty, there would be little need for firms to exist. However, economic activities are inherently difficult to price. It is the uncertainty surrounding the pricing of economic activities at each stage of production that provides an incentive for firms to organize. Firms eliminate the need for these market transactions. They simplify the process of producing goods and services using an entrepreneur or executive team to direct the firm's resources and activities.

As long as firms can produce goods and services more efficiently than market mechanisms, they will continue to grow in size until the cost of organizing additional activities internally exceeds the cost of performing the same activities on the open market. Therefore, firms and markets are alternative mechanisms for managing economic activities.[6] Oliver Williamson from the University of Pennsylvania extended this view by explaining that corporations are the product of "a series of organizational innovations that have had the purpose and effect of economizing on transaction costs."[7] He pointed to the development of the line-and-staff organization, selective forward integration of manufacturers into distribution, the development of the multidivisional corporate form, and appearance of the multinational enterprise as examples of organizational inventions that have increased the efficient allocation and distribution of economic resources.

The work of Alfred Chandler is also worth noting because it provided insight into how firms manage growth and diversification. He documented the evolving strategies and structures of General Motors, E. I. du Pont de Nemours, Standard Oil of New Jersey, and Sears Roebuck and Company during the twentieth century.[8] He found that, as these firms grew larger over time, it became more difficult for executives to efficiently manage the growing complexities of multiple businesses. They managed this growing complexity by creating semiautonomous operating divisions that were organized along product and geographic lines. Each division was then led by executives with expertise in the area. This organizational design became known as the divisional structure or M-form. Chandler's work led to the notion that "structure follows strategy." As firms adopt new strategies, they must reorganize their organizational structures and processes that support the new strategies.

Why Do Firms Internalize Economic Activities?

Why do firms vertically integrate supply and distribution activities instead of buying components from outside suppliers or contracting distribution activities to outside firms? If firms could outsource component purchases, labor, distribution, and other value-chain activities at low cost and risk, there would be little incentive for firms to vertically integrate. Contracting, however, can be both risky and costly. For example, contractors often engage in opportunistic behavior, such as what might occur when a distributor actively promotes another company's accounts at the expense of the firm's own accounts. Vertically integrating distribution activities may be the most reliable way of servicing the firm's accounts under such circumstances.

A second issue surrounds the problem of bounded rationality—the limited ability of individuals to formulate and solve complex problems.[9] It is more difficult for firms to control successive stages of a complex production process when outside contractors perform one or more functions. This explains why firms tend to integrate vertically during the early stages of an industry's life when product functionality is still uncertain. A good example is the computer industry. Computers had poor functionality when they were introduced in the late 1970s and early 1980s. It was leading semiconductors manufacturers of the day, such as IBM and Texas Instruments, that were the first to establish competitive positions in computers.

By integrating computer design and manufacturing with their existing semiconductor operations, these firms' own engineers and designers could work together to resolve product functionality issues between the computer and its components. By the late 1980s, computer technologies had become largely standardized. Product functionality problems had also been sufficiently resolved that the basis of competition shifted from product functionality to reliability and brand. This motivated the entry of new firms into both the semiconductor and computer industries and supported firm specialization at different stages of the value chain. Vertical integration was no longer a necessary or efficient method of designing and assembling computers.

Vertical integration is, therefore, an important mechanism for increasing the quality of the production process when the use of outside contractors is either too costly or is an ineffective means of resolving functionality and technology problems. The same processes are at work when the firm diversifies into different product lines. Diversification is a means of capturing integration economies associated with the sharing of value-chain activities across different businesses. Economies of scope efficiencies are achieved when it is less costly to jointly produce two or more products than to produce them using separate production processes.

Diversification, however, does not always lead to scope efficiencies. David Teece from Stanford's Graduate School of Business showed that the joint production of two products in a single firm is not always less costly than the independent production of products by two different firms.[10] Firms can achieve economies of scale efficiencies by specializing in the production of a single product. Therefore, it is possible for two specialized firms to have lower cost functions than a single firm that produces multiple products in the same production process. That is, economies of scale and scope are sometimes alternative ways of achieving synergies. When firm specialization allows independent firms to produce product components at lower cost, then it becomes advantageous for firms to purchase those components using market transactions rather than producing them inside the firm.

Diversification becomes a profitable strategy when it is undesirable to freely trade inputs. Two inputs are important—technological know-how and specialized and indivisible physical assets. If know-how is freely traded among firms, it takes the form of a public good. The know-how becomes freely available to all consumers, and the creator of the know-how receives nothing in return for its investment. In order to prevent its investments in innovation and technology from appropriation by other firms, a firm must internalize its technological know-how. The firm benefits by leveraging its know-how across multiple businesses.

"Any asset which yields scale economies can similarly provide the foundation for scope economies if it serves as an input into two or more production processes."[11] If a machine or production process leads to scale efficiencies with greater production, and the machine or production process can also be used to perform a second function, then the firm can simultaneously achieve scale and scope efficiencies. The same result occurs when the firm internalizes its know-how. When a firm such as Honda leverages its specialized knowledge in small engine manufacturing to diversify into other product areas (e.g., boat engines, lawn mowers, and home generators), it is able to achieve both scale and scope efficiencies. The ability to continue to generate profits from these competencies, however, rests on its ability to prevent competitors from imitating the same competencies.

Why Do Firms Engage in M&As?

What factors determine whether a firm should acquire or develop new businesses internally? The firm is influenced by both industry and firm characteristics. The early work of George Yip from the London Business School provides good insight into how firms make these decisions.[12] He found that six factors are significant: (a) industry growth rate, (b) investment intensity (e.g., capital costs), (c) size of the target company's parent, (d) level of diversification of the acquiring firm, (e) market growth prospects, and (f) competitive position of the target company.

Entry Barriers and the Market Growth Rate

Companies are more likely to acquire other businesses when the market growth rate has slowed. Most mature businesses have strong, well-established competitors that can be expected to retaliate against new entrants. At the same time, a declining market growth rate normally leads to consolidation as weaker competitors are acquired by stronger ones. Internally developing new products adds capacity to an already mature market. Therefore, acquisition is the preferred strategy for entering the industry for the first time or strengthening the firm's existing competitive position.

Investment Intensity

Companies are more likely to acquire other businesses when industry capital costs are low. This finding may seem counter intuitive. When fixed costs are high, established competitors are likely to possess scale advantages that force new entrants to enter the industry at a cost disadvantage. New entrants are forced to operate at a loss until they are able to increase revenues to cover high break-even fixed costs. High fixed costs also translate into higher exit costs for existing competitors. This means that established firms can be expected to defend their competitive positions more aggressively. If potential retaliation of existing competitors and scale disadvantages are viewed as significant entry barriers, then one might expect acquisition to be a more effective means of overcoming these entry barriers.

However, low fixed costs also mean that market entry is less costly. Therefore, low fixed-cost industries attract more new entrants than high fixed-cost industries. Lower capital costs reduce the potential loss of diversification strategies and encourage firms with excess cash flow to diversify into these industries. In contrast, high fixed-cost industries such as automobiles, chemicals, semiconductors, and computers have well established competitors with strong cash flows. New products are more likely to be introduced by existing competitors that develop new products internally in these industries.

Size of the Target's Parent Company

Companies are more likely to acquire other businesses when existing companies have large parents. Incumbent firms can mount more aggressive defenses against new market entrants when they can draw on parent company resources. This problem is exacerbated when the firm trying to enter the industry is small relative to both incumbent firms and incumbent firms' parents. In such cases, acquisition is a preferred market entry strategy.

Diversification Experience

Companies with diversified parents are more likely to enter new markets through acquisition rather than internal development. Diversified firms have greater acquisition experience relative to nondiversifiers. This experience can be leveraged in subsequent acquisitions. The knowledge-based view of the firm suggests that firms that possess acquisition capabilities are more successful making acquisitions compared to firms without similar capabilities.[13] Acquirers learn how to manage organizational processes through experiences and over time. Acquirers that are able to accumulate experiences from past acquisitions often perform at higher levels and have higher merger survival rates in later acquisitions.[14]

In many acquisitions, experience is accumulated by individual executives involved in an acquisition. Unless the same executives are involved in subsequent acquisitions, this experience may never be transferred to other executives. As a result, companies that engage in frequent acquisitions may show wide variability in merger integration success from one acquisition to another. They fail to translate the accumulated experiences of individual executives and employees into organizational competencies. The most successful acquirers are those that codify their knowledge in ways that allow the firm to duplicate past successes in future acquisitions. Examples include quantitative models for financial analysis, product mapping, self-training, and project management. It also includes such simple tools as due diligence checklists and due diligence, systems training, and integration manuals.[15]

Market Growth Prospects

Companies are more likely to acquire businesses in industries that demonstrate immediate market potential. In contrast, markets that have long-term growth potential but are not currently profitable are more attractive to established competitors. Because they are committed to an industry over the long term, existing firms are more likely to have strong investment programs that are designed to develop future products to replace existing products as they mature.

Target Company's Competitive Position

Companies are more likely to acquire businesses when their entry into a new industry is expected to result in a weak competitive position. Weaker competitors are more likely to have attractive acquisition prices that justify purchase premiums. In addition, acquirers may be attracted to businesses when they can use internal resources and capabilities to improve the company's performance and competitive position.

Do M&As Create Value?

When executives are asked to comment on their own acquisitions, most answer that their acquisitions create value for shareholders and that the company's strategic objectives have been met. The evidence, however, suggests that a large portion of M&As—one-half or more—fail to live up to expectations.[16] In addition, about one-half of all acquired companies are divested by the parent within 5 years.[17]

Four methods are generally used to evaluate the success of M&As: (a) analysis of stock market returns to target and acquiring company shareholders following the merger announcement ("event studies"), (b) analysis of target company performance after the merger using accounting measures such as return on assets (ROA), (c) surveys of executives involved in M&As, and (d) case studies of individual acquisitions. In his book *Applied Mergers & Acquisitions*, Robert F. Bruner, dean of the Darden Graduate School of Business at the University of Virginia, provides a comprehensive summary and discussion of the findings of studies in each of these four areas.[18] Event studies and accounting measures of performance are the most reliable methods of examining merger performance because they rely on large sample sizes and follow rigorous scientific guidelines. In contrast, surveys of executives and case studies provide descriptive information about individual mergers but generally cannot be used to draw conclusions about the success or failure of acquisition strategies.

Empirical studies of stock market returns show that the stock value of target company shareholders increases significantly—an average of 30% over market returns—immediately following an acquisition announcement. The results of studies of the stock returns to shareholders of the acquiring firm, however, have been mixed. Bruner analyzed the results of 54 studies. Of these, 22 studies (40.7%) reported negative returns to shareholders. Thirty-two studies (59.3%) reported positive returns. He concluded that returns to shareholders in the acquiring firm are essentially zero (i.e., investors earn required returns but no more).[19] The majority of studies, however, reported positive combined returns. This suggests that M&As do pay when one considers the combined stock market performance of shareholders in both firms. In a more recent meta-analysis of 93 empirical studies of M&A performance, King, Dalton, Daily, and Covin[20] concluded that stock returns to shareholders in acquiring firms following the announcement of an acquisition are either insignificant or negative. Indeed, accounting measures of performance such as ROA, return on equity (ROE), and return on sales (ROS) are generally not improved in target companies following an acquisition.[21]

Conclusion

Thus, the expectation of synergies that may exist at the time of an acquisition announcement are not realized in most acquisitions. The conclusion is that shareholders do not receive higher than normal gains from holding stock in acquiring companies that grow through acquisition. When faced with the choice of receiving cash or stock in an acquisition, target company shareholders would be better off taking cash in lieu of stock in the acquiring company. Continuing to hold equity in the acquiring company is likely to produce insignificant or negative gains compared to the market as a whole.

CHAPTER 5

Why Mergers Fail

I still don't understand why the acquirer paid such a high premium to acquire us. Their management was not forthright when they made assurances that our executives would be retained. They also weren't forthright when they discussed where they wanted our company to be positioned. I was initially excited when I was asked to head the new division. I viewed it as a great opportunity. However, the new parent never gave us the proper technology or adequate resources to successfully build the business. I overstayed my welcome. It was time to try something else. I asked for an offer allowing me to leave. The offer was to my satisfaction so I left.

—Chief executive describing his experience after his company was acquired

Determining a Purchase Price

Michael Porter at Harvard Business School suggests that corporate strategy rarely creates value unless it passes three tests: (a) the cost-of-entry test, (b) the better-off test, and (c) the attractiveness test (see Figure 5.1).[1] Merger success depends on the acquiring company not overpaying for the target (i.e., paying a price that does not capitalize future cash flows from the acquisition). Theoretically, it is impossible for acquiring firms

- **The cost-of-entry test**
  - ➤ Purchase premiums don't capitalize future cash flows.

- **The better-off test**
  - ➤ Performance of the parent and/or target company is enhanced through value transfer.

- **The attractiveness test**
  - ➤ The target company's industry has a favorable industry structure that contributes to corporate performance.

Figure 5.1. Corporate strategy tests

Source: Porter (1987).

to benefit from acquisitions in an efficient market. When analysts and shareholders have access to the same information as managers, it is assumed that they will bid up the price of the target company until the purchase price exactly offsets expected future cash flows from the acquisition. That is, the purchase price will be bid up until the net present value from the acquisition is zero. In this instance, acquiring firm shareholders will earn an acceptable profit from the acquisition but no more. If capital markets are, indeed, efficient, then it is reasonable to assume that some portion of acquiring firms overpay for the companies they acquire.

It is common for firms to assess the potential economic value of an acquisition using the discounted cash flow method. The firm forecasts future cash flows from the acquisition—typically over a 10-year period—and discounts them by the company's cost of capital in order to calculate an estimated present value of future cash flows. The maximum purchase price the firm can pay and still make a profit is equal to the present value of expected future cash flows—a purchase price that exactly offsets future cash flows from the acquisition and results in a projected net present value of zero. A purchase that yields a net present value of zero represents a break-even investment; that is, the return on the investment is equal to the firm's risk-adjusted cost of capital.

The discounted cash flow method or "shareholder value" approach was popularized by Alfred Rappaport from Northwestern University's Kellogg School of Management in his book *Creating Shareholder Value*.[2] Rappaport argued that accounting measures of performance such as earnings per share (EPS) and return on investment (ROI) are misleading indicators of firm performance because they don't measure changes in shareholder value. For example, accounting measures of performance do not incorporate risk or inflation. They do not consider the effect on earnings from the use of different accounting methods. They do not consider dividend policy. And they ignore the time value of money, among other factors.[3] Therefore, reported earnings and actual increases or decreases in stock value are often not correlated. As a result, firms can grow earnings without concomitantly increasing the firm's stock value. The discounted cash flow method of valuing investments, however, is also fraught with problems. In particular, it is difficult to accurately project future cash flows from an investment because it is inherently difficult to accurately predict the future value of variables that affect performance. The task of estimating future cash flows is somewhat less problematic when an investment is made in tangibles such as physical plant, property, or equipment. It is far more problematic when an investment is made in intangible assets such as new technologies, know-how, and brand equity (see Table 5.1). Many firms invest aggressively in research and development (R&D) to develop new technologies or in advertising to increase brand equity. When firms invest in R&D or advertising, current earnings are sacrificed to create opportunities to produce future income.

Intangible investments are a double-edged sword. On the one hand, investments made to develop intangible resources and capabilities are risky and costly because future income streams are unpredictable. On the other hand, a competitive advantage based on intangible investments in brand equity or new technologies is far more difficult for a competitor to imitate. A competitive advantage based on investments in tangible assets such as physical plant, property, and equipment is generally easier for competitors to imitate. The most successful firms tend to make intangible investments for this reason. Competitive advantages based on intangible resources and capabilities are more sustainable over time when they are unique, durable, difficult to transfer from one firm to another, and are difficult for competitors to replicate.[4]

Those who believe in the efficiency of markets assume that shareholders have access to the same information as executives. In such cases,

Table 5.1. Resources and Capabilities

Resources		
Tangible	Intangible	Human
• Cash • Borrowing capacity • Land • Mineral reserves • Physical plant	• Patents • Trade secrets • Brand • Reputation • Corporate culture	• Know-how • Skills • Talent
Capabilities		
Corporate strategy	Innovation & operations	Marketing and distribution
• Management • Corporate coordination • Global management • Mergers & acquisitions	• Innovation & technology • Product design • Low-cost manufacturing • Flexible manufacturing	• Brand management • Advertising • Distribution • Responsiveness

shareholders in the target company are able to develop similar estimates of the future value of an acquisition as executives in the bidding firm. Consequently, the target company's stock should be bid up to the point at which the purchase price capitalizes all future value from the acquisition. There may be, however, instances where executives have information about potential future gains from an acquisition that is unknown to shareholders. When one considers the companies listed on *Fortune* magazine's annual "World's Most Admired Companies" list (e.g., Apple, Berkshire Hathaway, Toyota, Google, Johnson & Johnson, Procter & Gamble, Fedex, Southwest Airlines, General Electric, and Microsoft), it is apparent that much of the value in these companies stems from these firms' intangible assets, know-how, capabilities, and cumulative brand equity.[5] As firms focus their investments on developing intangible resources and capabilities, it becomes increasingly difficult to accurately value acquisitions—both for bidding firms and shareholders. This difficulty may partially explain why some acquiring firms pay premiums for target companies in excess of what shareholders view as the break-even purchase price from the investment.

The Tendency to Overpay in Acquisitions

When the first edition of Rappaport's book was published in 1986, it was required reading for all PepsiCo managers. We were all given a copy. It became a basis for our own valuations of acquisition candidates. We analyzed all acquisition candidates using a 12-year cash flow model that calculated the acquisition's net present value, as well as its ROI and payback in years. We judged potential acquisitions on the basis of all three measures. One of my responsibilities as manager of strategic planning at Kentucky Fried Chicken in the late 1980s was to analyze potential acquisitions in Latin America. PepsiCo used a matrix organizational structure, and I simultaneously reported to the vice president of international finance (Bob Briggs, who later left PepsiCo to become president of Arby's International) and the vice president for Latin America (Guillermo Heredia, who later left PepsiCo to become president and chief operating officer of Aeromexico).

At that time, we were in a battle for market share with Burger King in Puerto Rico. Puerto Rico was rapidly becoming a saturated market. Therefore, building new restaurants to match Burger King's new restaurant openings merely kept us at parity. It also added restaurant capacity to the market and cannibalized sales from our other restaurants. An opportunity arose to acquire Church's restaurant chains in Puerto Rico. This acquisition would have allowed us to nearly double market share over night. Church's had annual sales of approximately $30 million. Guillermo decided to fly to Puerto Rico to meet with Church's franchise owners. Beforehand, he asked me what kind of purchase price we might consider. I responded that it was difficult to give him a number without first seeing Church's financial statements. However, we often used a "one-time first-year sales" estimate for inside discussions of potential acquisitions. Using this philosophy, we began thinking of Church's in terms of a potentially $30 million purchase. This was a rough method of valuation, but it wasn't intended to be used in outside discussions. Rather, it was designed to give us a means of beginning discussions within the company before we broached negotiations with an outside party. I added to Guillermo that I would not mention this number in his first meeting.

However, Guillermo did mention it. Two weeks later, we received copies of Church's financial statements, and what I saw shocked me. Church's had no assets! They were leasing their land, buildings, and equipment. Based on their financial statements, my cash flow analysis showed that this acquisition would yield a net present value of zero at a purchase price of no more than $12 million! I can only imagine the excitement that spread among Church's owners when they heard $30 million mentioned as a possible selling price!

We immediately initiated what became known as "Operation Iglesias" (Operation Church's). We spent the next 2 months figuring out ways of inflating our revenue estimates and deflating our costs, in order to move up the purchase price. As a young manager, I was dismayed by the entire process. It was clear that we were producing fictional numbers to support an acquisition championed by a single executive. Our final analysis boosted the break-even purchase price to $24 million—more than twice what I considered to be the true value of the acquisition!

Soon after, the chief financial officer from PepsiCo headquarters flew to Louisville to listen to Guillermo's presentation of the potential acquisition. Afterward, he looked at me and said, "Jeff, how much do you think Church's is really worth?" I thought for a few seconds, looked at him and said, "$12 million." He grinned and replied, "You're probably right, but if Guillermo wants to buy Church's, let him go ahead with it and if it fails, he'll have to answer for it." In the end, Church's rejected our offer. They were so mesmerized by the initial figure of $30 million floated at the first meeting that they wouldn't consider selling for anything less.

Creating Synergies in a Merger

Merger Value Creation: The "Better-Off Test"

Mergers and acquisitions (M&As) benefit shareholders when value is transferred between merging firms in ways that enhance the combined performance of the merging firms. Either the acquiring firm transfers value to the target company that increases its performance or the target company provides something of value to the acquirer that increases the acquirer's performance. This value transfer is often referred to as synergy creation: 2 + 2 = 5. Synergy creation depends on a variety of factors such as the financial and strategic fit between merging firms. The existence of potential synergies, however, is not a guarantee that synergies will actually be realized.[6] Many mergers fail because of poor candidate selection, an inability to realize projected economies of scale and scope efficiencies, or because of unforeseen changes in competition.[7] Moreover, a poor organizational fit between the two firms can create culture clashes that prevent effective integration, even when strong financial and strategic fits are present.[8]

Executives commonly cite potential efficiency gains in order to justify an acquisition. There are, however, a range of reasons why executives engage in M&As. Friedrich Trautwein, chairman of SMT Scharf AG, a worldwide leader in the design and management of mining railway systems, published a comprehensive review of strategic management research on merger motives.[9] His review is shown in Figure 5.2. He outlined seven theories of merger motives: (a) efficiency theory, (b) valuation theory, (c) empire-building theory, (d) process theory, (e) raider theory, (f) monopoly theory, and (g) disturbance theory. Efficiency theory tops the list as the most popular of all theories. Efficiency gains from a merger are often broken into three areas:

1. *Operational synergies.* Consolidating value-chain activities to create economies of scale as well as scope efficiencies. Operational synergies are also created when know-how is transferred across value-chain activities to lower costs or enhance product value. An often cited example is Philip Morris's (now Altria) acquisition of Miller Brewing from W. R. Grace in 1969. Philip Morris outbid PepsiCo for Miller, paying $130 million. Despite operating in different industries, Philip Morris transferred its brand managers into Miller's organization to improve its marketing capabilities. The result was a significant increase in Miller's market share. Twenty-three years later, in 2002, Philip Morris sold Miller Brewing to South African Breweries (SAB) for $5.6 billion.

2. *Financial synergies.* Lowering the firm's systematic risk by investing in a diversified portfolio of unrelated businesses. It has also been argued that acquisitions help the firm create an internal capital market. This market gives the company access to lower-cost capital and creates superior performance through more efficient allocation of capital among business units. While research does show that size is an advantage in capital markets, there is little evidence to support the premise that firms can either (a) lower systematic risk or (b) create superior internal capital markets that shareholders cannot achieve themselves by holding a diversified portfolio of stocks.[10]

3. *Managerial synergies.* Transferring superior acquiring company management skills into the target company to improve its performance.

Despite its widespread use to justify M&As, efficiency theory has received only modest support. As discussed in chapter 4, target company shareholders are the primary winners in M&As. The value of target company stock generally increases significantly following a merger announcement. This tendency suggests that the market anticipates synergy gains from the merger. However, the value of acquiring firm stock generally does not increase. This fact suggests that the market believes that any potential value from the acquisition is offset by the purchase price paid by the acquirer. Market psychology may also be a factor.

- **Efficiency theory**
  - ➤ M&As create operational, financial, and managerial efficiencies.

- **Valuation theory**
  - ➤ Executives have superior information about a target's true value.

- **Empire-building theory**
  - ➤ Executives acquire other firms to maximize their own wealth and power.

- **Process theory**
  - ➤ Executives make acquisitions based on criteria other than rational analysis.

- **Raider theory**
  - ➤ Raiders bid on firms as a means of extracting wealth from shareholders.

- **Monopoly theory**
  - ➤ Acquisitions increase the firm's monopoly power.

- **Disturbance theory**
  - ➤ Acquisitions are the result of macroeconomic influences.

Figure 5.2. Mergers motives

Source: Trautwein (1990).

Valuation theory suggests that acquiring firm executives may possess better information about the value of an acquisition than the market. This rationale might explain why executives are willing to pay higher purchase premiums. The problem is that executives, even when in possession of superior information, would still bid the price of the target up to the point where future gains are capitalized by the purchase price.

Managerial Empire Building

One reason that firms may overpay for target companies is that some executives may champion acquisitions as a means of empire building—increasing the assets and employees under their control to increase their personal wealth, power, and potential for advancement.[11] Michael Jensen at Harvard University argued that executives rarely distribute excess cash flows to shareholders in the form of dividends. Doing so would signal to shareholders that they are unable to find investments that deliver greater returns than shareholders could earn on their own by investing in a diversified stock portfolio. Instead, executives use excess cash flows to invest in acquisitions that increase the span of their own control, even though such investments may be risky or deliver subpar returns. Many in the news media have promoted this view of executives, especially in light of recent corporate scandals (e.g., Enron, Tyco, and AIG). Empire-building theory has received significant support in strategic management research.

Impediments to Rational Decision Making

Empire-building theory is similar to process theory in that both argue that executives may overpay for acquisitions for reasons other than rational analysis. Whereas empire-building theory suggests that executives overpay as a means of promoting their own wealth and power, process theory suggests that executives overpay because they make decisions on factors other than rational analysis. This overpayment may occur for a variety of reasons. Executives may be overly optimistic about the positive outcome of an acquisition or overestimate their ability to integrate an acquisition.

In other instances, executives may find it difficult to accurately analyze a potential acquisition because of information overload or because of the complexity of the analysis.[12] To deal with uncertainty and an abundance of information, managers may use cognitive simplifying practices to make decisions.[13] One way that executives deal with complexity is to delegate data gathering and analysis to subordinates. They may also outsource analysis to outside analysts such as investment bankers and consultants. The result may be an incomplete understanding of costs and benefits of the proposed acquisition. Poor planning, political pressures, escalating commitment to an acquisition, and a failure to accurately analyze all costs and benefits often leads to poor decisions and decisions to pay too much.[14]

In developing his "hubris hypothesis of corporate takeovers," Richard Roll from UCLA's Graduate School of Business argued that many executives make errors because they overestimate their own expertise.[15] He called the tendency of executives to proceed with an ill-advised acquisition as managerial overoptimism or the "winner's curse." Based on successes in past acquisitions, executives become overconfident about their own abilities and bid more for the target than rational bidders under similar circumstances. Thus, psychology plays an important role in explaining why executives make poor decisions and why they overpay for acquisitions.

Monopoly Theory and Industry Structure

Monopoly theory provides another view of merger motives. Executives acquire other firms to increase their market power. Acquisitions increase the firm's size and control over resources. Size enables firms to achieve greater economies of scale, which lowers costs and increases profit margins. Economies of scale are also an important barrier to the entry of new firms, which are forced to enter the industry at a significant cost disadvantage relative to established firms. In addition to scale advantages, acquisitions allow firms to support the development of new products and to use profits from existing products and markets to subsidize entry into new markets.

As industries mature, they tend to consolidate around a smaller number of larger competitors. Acquisitions enable firms to increase market share by acquiring weaker competitors without adding new capacity to the industry. As industries consolidate, competitors often recognize their mutual interdependence and pursue competitive strategies that avoid direct price competition. Price competition typically leads to price wars that destroy the profitability of all firms in the industry. This explains why competitors in industries such as breakfast cereals (e.g., Kellogg's and General Mills) and soft drinks (e.g., Coca-Cola and Pepsi-Cola) focus on advertising that strengthens brand loyalty among existing consumers. Focusing advertising on efforts to convince a competitor's customers to switch loyalties merely encourages retaliatory advertising by the firm's competitors.

The "Attractiveness Test"

Corporate performance is determined by three primary drivers: (a) the firm's executive team, (b) firm strategy, and (c) the structure of the firm's industry.[16] As Table 5.2 demonstrates, each industry has a unique structure or set of economic characteristics that influences its profitability. Firms—including today's industry leaders—will tend to regress toward the mean level of performance in their industry over time. Therefore, firms that diversify into other industries must consider whether the target industry has an attractive structure and whether overall corporate performance might change with changes in their business portfolios.

Strategy research indicates that between 20% and 30% of a firm's profitability is determined by the structure of its industry.[17] Therefore, corporate diversification strategies lead to changes in corporate-level performance when the firm acquires other firms that operate in different

Table 5.2. Profitability of U.S. Industries

Profit as % of revenues—2007					
Network equipment	28.8	Food services	7.9	Packaging, containers	5.5
Mining, crude oil	23.8	Publishing, printing	7.9	Wholesalers: diversified	4.3
Pharmaceuticals	15.8	Utilities: gas & electric	7.9	Specialty retailers	3.8
Medical products	15.2	Industrial & farm equip.	7.6	Energy	3.7
Oil & gas equipment	13.7	Electronics	7.6	Airlines	3.6
Commercial banks	12.6	Hotels, casinos	7.3	General merchandise	3.5
Railroads	12.4	Aerospace and defense	7.2	Health care facilities	3.3
Entertainment	12.4	Beverages	7.2	Pipelines	3.1
Insurance: life	10.6	Chemicals	7.0	Engineering, construction	2.8
Household products	10.2	Internet services	7.0	Pharmacies	2.6
Securities	10.1	Food consumer prod.	6.5	Food and drug stores	2.1
Insurance: P&C	9.9	Telecommunications	6.4	Automotive retailing	1.1
Real estate	9.9	Health care insurance	6.2	Motor vehicles and parts	1.1
Scientific equipment	9.8	Petroleum refining	6.0	Semiconductors	0.6
Financial data service	8.7	Computers	5.5	Diversified financial svcs.	-0.9

Source: Fortune (2008).

industries. Industry structure, however, may have different implications for bidding firms depending on their relative competitive advantages. Highly efficient firms that have strong cost advantages may, for example, be in a position to price at a premium. In the process, they maximize their own profits and, at the same time, increase the overall level of industry profitability. Inefficient firms with higher cost structures, in contrast, may be able to profit in industries that are growing at a rapid pace, since demand exceeds supply and competition is weak. Therefore, what may be viewed as an "attractive" industry to one firm may be viewed as "unattractive" by another firm.[18]

CHAPTER 6

Executive Turnover and Postmerger Performance

I was a person who didn't drink. To be an executive in the acquiring firm (alcoholic beverage company) and not drink was a no-no. I was told that if I didn't drink at corporate functions, I would never fit in.

   After several months, I was replaced as vice president of marketing and given a desk job. Six months later, I was told to take a retirement package or a 40% cut in salary that year, which would be followed by another 33% salary cut the following year. The message was clear. After 35 years with the company, I quit.

—Vice president of a company acquired by a beverage firm,
describing why he left 1 year after the acquisition

Does Executive Turnover After an Acquisition Lead to Lower Performance? The Current Evidence

Is the departure of a significant portion of a target company's top management team shortly after an acquisition associated with lower postmerger performance? Most people think so. Walsh's initial study in 1988 demonstrated that turnover rates in acquired top management teams are significantly higher than normal turnover rates.[1] A variety of studies, including my own research, have found similar results. A long stream of literature going back 20 years now shows that mergers and acquisitions (M&As) can be tumultuous for target company executives.

   But does the departure of executives from the target company really matter? Before 1993, no study had directly analyzed the association between executive turnover and postmerger performance. Many scholars did, however, believe that there was an association. On the one hand, scholars argued that acquisitions are a consequence of bad management—poorly managed firms become takeover targets precisely because they are badly managed. In such cases, terminating target company executives should have a positive effect on postmerger performance.[2] On the other hand, scholars argued that executives are important resources that are critical to the success of an acquisition.[3] Executives are often difficult to replace. As a result, executive departures are likely to harm performance.[4]

The first evidence that executive turnover may be associated with lower postmerger performance was reported in two studies published in 1993 by Donald Hambrick (The Pennsylvania State University) and Bert Cannella (Tulane University).[5] In both studies, they analyzed the post-merger performance of 96 large, publicly traded U.S. companies acquired between 1980 and 1984. Executive turnover was calculated as the portion of executives employed at the time of the acquisition who had departed by the end of the second year following the acquisition. Performance was measured using surveys sent to executives in the acquiring firm and secu-rity analysts who specialized in the target firm's industry.

Each survey respondent was asked to rate the performance of the acquired company at the time of the acquisition and 4 years after the acquisition. The respondents' ratings of premerger performance were highly correlated with the target company's premerger return on equity (ROE). This finding suggested that the survey estimates of post-merger performance in the target company accurately represented actual performance.

The results of Cannella and Hambrick's two studies can be summa-rized as follows:

1. Average performance of the 96 companies in the sample improved following the acquisition. That is, average performance in year 4 improved relative to average performance at the time of the acquisition.
2. An average of 50% of the target firms' executives departed by the second year following the acquisition.
3. Turnover in year 2 was negatively related to performance in year 4. This finding suggested that higher turnover led to lower postmerger performance.
4. The departure of more senior executives was related to significantly lower postmerger performance. This performance decline suggested that more senior executives are especially important to the successful integration of target firms.

5. Relatedness between the two firms was not related to differences in either performance levels or levels of departure.

6. Premerger performance was not correlated with postmerger performance. This finding supported the notion that acquisitions are disruptive to ongoing strategies. Acquisitions promote performance discontinuity.

7. All firms in the sample showed overall regression toward the mean level of performance. Firms with low premerger performance tended to improve after the acquisition. Firms with high premerger performance tended to deteriorate after the acquisition.

8. Performance changes in the group of firms with low executive turnover were superior to performance changes in the group of firms with high executive turnover. Firms with high levels of performance before the acquisition that experienced high turnover among target company executives after the acquisition experienced a greater deterioration in performance than other firms, especially those with lower executive turnover rates.

In sum, these studies suggest that executives matter in acquisitions. Acquiring firms that make an effort to retain target company executives should be rewarded with higher postmerger performance in the acquired firm.

Similar results were suggested in a study by Hema Krishnan (Xavier University), Alex Miller (University of Tennessee), and William Judge (Old Dominion University) in 1997.[6] They sampled 147 of the largest publicly traded U.S. firms acquired between 1986 and 1988. They measured postmerger performance based on return on assets (ROA) of the acquiring company 3 years after the acquisition. They measured turnover based on the proportion of the target company's top management team in place at the time of the acquisition that had left by the end of the third year following the acquisition.

Their study differed from Cannella and Hambrick's studies in two ways. First, they analyzed postmerger performance of the acquiring firm rather than the target firm. Second, they measured performance based on accounting measures of performance (ROA) rather than surveys of executives' and analysts' perceptions of target company performance.

They found a significant negative relationship between turnover and performance. Thus, their findings were consistent with the findings of Cannella and Hambrick. The higher the level of departures among target company executives through the third year following the acquisition, the lower the level of acquiring company ROA in the third year following the acquisition. They argued that these results demonstrated that stability among top executives in the target company is critical to the postmerger integration process.

Based on existing research, several points can be made regarding the effect of target company executive turnover:

1. When target executives depart, they take with them firm- and industry-specific knowledge that may be difficult to replace. This knowledge often makes it more difficult for acquiring firms to successfully integrate the target firm, which may lead to lower performance in the acquired firm.

2. Departures of target company executives may also harm the performance of the acquiring firm. The acquiring firm must fill any void left by departing executives with its own resources and executives. Moreover, it must commit more time and effort to integration efforts. Doing so may deprive the acquiring company of resources and capabilities necessary to support its own ongoing operations.

3. When target company executives depart, executives in the acquiring firm must deal directly with middle and lower-level managers in the target company. They must also establish cooperative relationships with these managers and employees. This process takes time and may affect ongoing strategic projects and may also create uncertainties and anxieties among target employees that affect integration efforts and performance.

4. Acquiring firm executives who are transferred into the target company tend to be viewed as outsiders. Many target employees resent their presence. Morale and commitment to the newly merged company is often negatively affected and many employees choose to leave as a result.

The conclusions of the three studies described earlier have since been widely accepted among both academics and practitioners. Target company executive turnover following a merger or acquisition is now generally believed to be detrimental to corporate performance. Moreover, executive turnover is believed to cause performance to decline in both the target company and the combined entity. Subsequent studies have focused on identifying the causes of this high turnover, their objective being to determine how organizations can increase retention of executives after an acquisition. I discuss these studies in greater detail in chapter 7.

Does Executive Turnover After an Acquisition Lead to Lower Performance? A Contrary View

Over the past several years, I have updated and expanded my database on executive turnover to include more than 1,000 firms. It follows the career paths of more than 23,000 executives over a 17-year period. It provides the foundation for analyses that are unlikely to be duplicated elsewhere simply because of the time and effort necessary to build a database of this magnitude and depth. I have found similarities but also important differences in turnover patterns based on merger, firm, and industry characteristics. My data suggest that industry structure, the culture of the merging firms, the application of technology, business fundamentals, and industry stage of development, among other factors, may significantly alter the desired composition of the new target company top management team following an acquisition. In short, *my research suggests that—contrary to conventional wisdom—a higher-than-average rate of executive turnover may actually be desirable in some acquisitions*. That is, executive turnover, rather than being harmful to performance, may be more or less desirable depending on a variety of factors. Organizations, as well as consulting firms engaged by organizations to help them manage the postmerger integration process, have generally accepted the premise that executive turnover leads to lower postmerger performance. As a result, many firms make efforts to retain executives following the acquisition. However, I believe that following such a strategy may cause some organizations to take steps that actually hurt postmerger integration efforts.

Rather than viewing the target company's top management team as a single unit that should be retained, acquiring firms should approach the integration process by matching key target company executives to roles in the newly merged firm that help maximize postmerger performance. In addition, they should focus on reestablishing leadership stability in the acquired firm, regardless of whether the integration strategy entails retaining key executives or terminating executives as a means of achieving greater efficiencies. In both cases, the goal should be to restore leadership continuity, without which long-term strategy execution will be difficult.

Is Performance Improved Following an Acquisition?

To answer this question, I retrieved a sample of 200 target companies from my database. Each of the target companies was acquired by a publicly traded firm. This allowed me to analyze performance effects. Target companies that were acquired more than once during the 5 years following their initial acquisition were excluded.

As the following graph shows, ROA for these 200 companies ranged from −28.04% to 27.30% during the year of the acquisition. Three years after the acquisition, ROA ranged from −95.24% to 105.95%. Clearly, acquisitions increased the variability in profitability among the acquiring firms. Some firms did significantly worse, others did significantly better. ROA actually decreased from an average of 3.44% to 2.90% between the year of the acquisition and 3 years after. This decrease suggests that M&As destroy shareholder value. However, 50.30% of the acquiring firms actually increased ROA following the acquisition. This finding is consistent with our existing thinking on M&As that about half of M&As fail to create value.

When we examine the midpoint rather than average ROA, we find that the midpoint of ROA for the acquiring firms increased from 3.37% to 3.91% during the 3 years following the acquisition. Thus, while some firms perform worse after an acquisition, those that succeed perform relatively better when compared to those firms that perform worse. We should conclude that mergers are risky strategies. For firms that handle postmerger issues poorly, M&As destroy significant shareholder value. However, for those acquiring firms that effectively integrate the firms they acquire, the benefits can be great.

In sum, M&As both destroy and create enormous wealth. Therefore, studies that uniformly conclude that M&As are a poor strategy because half of all M&As fail miss the point. When M&As are made for the right reasons and are integrated properly, they create enormous value for acquiring firms—often far more than could be created by developing new products and markets internally. The dilemma is in how acquiring firms seek out and integrate the companies they acquire.

Does Executive Turnover Really Lead to Lower Postmerger Performance?

No. My research shows no relationship between executive turnover in the target company after the acquisition and postmerger performance. Thus, my data do not support previous studies.

Further, my data show that premerger performance is related to postmerger performance, but only because high-performing acquirers start from a higher base. When I analyze the change in ROA during the 5 years after the acquisition, I find no relationship between pre- and postmerger performance. This finding *does* support existing studies. It suggests that

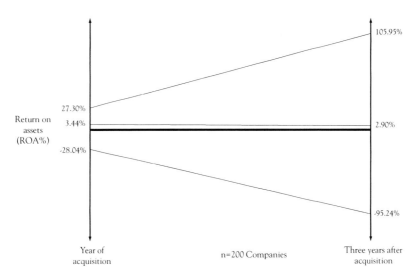

Figure 6.1. Performance effects of M&As

among employees that are detrimental to long-term performance. Therefore, retaining target executives—at least shortly following the acquisition—may be a critical component of long-term acquisition success.

At the same time, keeping executives too long may be equally detrimental to acquisition success. Many target company executives resist integration efforts of the acquiring firm. Retaining all executives may prevent the acquiring firm from taking full advantage of potential synergies. My research indicates that these effects dissipate by the fifth year after the acquisition.

CHAPTER 7

Before the Merger: Merger Motivations and Objectives

Our company was "put into play" by a hostile bidder. We were finally acquired by a friendly "White Knight." It was important to the acquirer to be perceived as honorable and all employment contracts and benefits were scrupulously honored.

However, they knew nothing about operating our business. They needed to retain our key people, despite strong incentives for many of our top executives to leave. Our top executives had vested employment contracts for lucrative "golden parachute" payments if we were acquired.

I stayed because I felt I was needed, there was plenty to do, I was well paid, and my welfare was considered by the new executive team.

—Top executive who decided to stay on after his
company was acquired by a "White Knight"

Merger Motives

Why do firms engage in mergers and acquisitions (M&As)? The answer to this question is clearly important. It determines the nature and extent of interactions between the two firms following the acquisition. It also determines the degree to which the firms' operations and value-chain activities will be integrated. The degree of integration, in turn, determines the resources and capabilities needed to successfully integrate the target company.

Target company executives are a key organizational resource. In many acquisitions, bidding firms are motivated to purchase another firm precisely because they would like to acquire management talent and capabilities. Executives may also have firm- and industry-specific knowledge that is essential to ongoing strategies. They may have strong relationships with employees and other stakeholder groups such as suppliers and customers. Good stakeholder relationships are important for negotiating favorable supplier contracts, controlling distribution quality, and maintaining customer satisfaction. Therefore, determining which target executives should be retained or replaced following the acquisition is a critical decision that has strong implications for integration success and long-term target company performance.

Numerous typologies have been developed to classify M&As. In 1980, the U.S. Federal Trade Commission (FTC) developed a classification system that remains in wide use today (see Figure 7.1).[1] A casual review of these categories makes it clear that not all M&As are the same. The motivations of M&As differ widely. Horizontal acquisitions, for example, involve the merger of two companies that sell the same product in the same geographic market—a milk producer in Buffalo that acquires a competing milk producer, for example. The objective in horizontal acquisitions is usually to increase market share and create economies of scale by spreading fixed costs across a larger revenue stream. Consolidating value-chain activities as a means of creating synergies often requires the elimination of redundant resources and assets.

Market extension acquisitions involve the merger of two firms that produce identical products or services but sell in different geographic markets. For example, a milk producer in Buffalo may acquire a milk producer in Philadelphia. Unlike horizontal acquisitions, which are designed to increase market share in existing markets, market extension acquisitions are designed to expand the firm's existing products and services into new markets. This type of acquisition may or may not involve the creation of economies of scale. For example, milk perishes quickly and is expensive to transport. Therefore, costs can only be contained—and

• **Horizontal:**
  ➢ Firms produce the same products in the same geographic markets.
• **Market extension:**
  ➢ Firms produce the same products in different geographic markets.
• **Product extension:**
  ➢ Firms produce and/or distribute similar products but do not compete directly.
• **Vertical:**
  ➢ Firms have a buyer-seller relationship.
• **Unrelated:**
  ➢ Firms produce unrelated products or services.

Figure 7.1. Merger categories—Federal Trade Commission

Source: U.S. Federal Trade Commission.

product quality maintained—by producing milk as close to the customer as possible. Thus, it may be difficult to create synergies by consolidating the target firm's physical plant, property, and equipment.

The manner in which the target company's top management team is managed may also differ from one acquisition to another. On the one hand, there may be opportunities to create synergies by eliminating redundant staff positions, which can be consolidated in the acquirer's headquarters. On the other hand, the acquirer may need target company expertise when it expands into geographic markets where it has little experience.

Product extension acquisitions involve the merging of firms that produce similar products and services but do not compete directly. An example is a milk producer that acquires a cheese producer. The creation of synergies by eliminating redundant positions or consolidating overlapping facilities may not be possible when the firm's products and services differ greatly. At the same time, the transfer of value from one firm to another is likely to depend on the relatedness that exists between the two firms' products and services, as well as the capabilities of both firms' top management teams.

Vertical acquisitions involve the merging of firms that control different stages of the same value chain. For example, a milk producer may acquire a grocery store. Such an acquisition may be motivated by a variety of goals, such as to control product quality, increase speed of distribution, or diversify into new product lines. Vertical acquisitions are similar to unrelated acquisitions, which involve the merger of firms that operate in different product areas. Because merging firms operate in different industry groups or operate in different stages of the value chain, firms may have very different sets of resources and capabilities. In these types of acquisitions, the creation of synergies is more difficult.

In sum, acquisitions are motivated by a variety of factors and involve the merging of different sets of resources and capabilities. Therefore, it is difficult to draw simplistic conclusions about how acquisitions should be integrated. More importantly, the desirability of retaining or replacing target company executives is likely to differ significantly from one acquisition to another, as well as from one firm to another.

Executive Perceptions of Merger Motives

When executives are asked about their primary motives for making acquisitions, they agree that the two most important objectives are to increase growth and market value of the firm.[2] Acquisitions provide a faster means of growth than internal development. In addition, acquisitions are viewed as a cheaper means of achieving growth objectives than building new plant, property, and equipment.

Table 7.1 shows a rank ordering of merger objectives by executives. The Xs reflect the perceptions of executives that a particular motive is more important in one or more of the three primary merger categories (horizontal, diversification, and unrelated mergers). Despite the similarity in objectives in terms of increasing firm growth and market value of the firm, there are differences in executives' perceptions across different merger types. For example, executives view horizontal mergers as an

Table 7.1. Executives' Perceptions of Merger Motives

#	Motive	Horizontal	Diversification	Unrelated
1	Increase firm growth		X	X
2	Increase economies of scale	X		
3	Increase market share	X		
4	Expand into new markets	X		
5	Increase market value of the firm		X	
6	Expand or improve product mix	X	X	X
7	Spread firm risk		X	X
8	Enhance firm power and reputation	X	X	
9	Invest excess capital			X
10	Acquire technical know-how		X	
11	Counter cyclical sales		X	
12	Acquire managerial talent		X	
13	Obtain tax advantages			X
14	Gain control over supply channels	X	X	
15	Defend against takeover		X	

Source: Baker, Miller, Thomas, and Ramsperger (1981).

important strategy for increasing economies of scale, increasing market share, and expanding into new markets. Product diversification is viewed as most important for increasing the growth of the firm, increasing market value of the firm, countering cyclical sales, and defending against takeover threats. In addition, diversification mergers are viewed as an important strategy for acquiring technological knowledge and management talent. Unrelated acquisitions are viewed as being a means of investing excess capital and obtaining tax advantages. Product extension and unrelated diversification acquisitions are viewed as having equally beneficial effects in spreading risk. In general, executives view product extension and unrelated acquisitions as much more similar in the objectives achieved when compared to horizontal acquisitions.

In sum, executives commonly view M&As as an important strategy for growing the firm over the long term. However, executives attach very different objectives to different merger types. Attempting to explain merger motivations using broad generalizations leads to an inaccurate picture of why executives engage in M&As.

Managerial Goals in Mergers and Acquisitions

A more sophisticated analysis of managerial goals was published by Gordon Walter and Jay Barney in 1990.[3] They conducted in-depth interviews with M&A specialists (e.g., investment bankers, venture capitalists, financial advisors, executives of underwriting firms, and corporate lawyers). Based on an analysis of merger motives in the academic literature, they developed a list of 20 managerial goals for M&As. They asked each specialist to rank the importance of each goal for five different categories of M&As. These categories included (a) M&As in general, (b) horizontal acquisitions, (c) concentric acquisitions, (d) vertical acquisitions, and (e) conglomerate acquisitions. The horizontal category included both horizontal and market extension acquisitions from the FTC categories. The concentric category is similar to the FTC's product extension acquisitions. Conglomerate acquisitions were defined as mergers between firms that had no buyer–seller relationship, had no technical or distribution relationships, and sold different products. They analyzed the rankings using cluster analysis to produce a taxonomy of M&A objectives.

Clearly, value can be transferred from the acquiring firm to the target, from the target firm to the acquirer, or between both companies (see Table 7.2). The direction of the value transfer determines which resources and capabilities—possessed by the acquirer, target, or both—will be the basis of value creation.

In the case of Cluster 1, economies of scale and scope are created by transferring skills, assets, or both from one firm to the other. This transfer requires that some assets be consolidated to create a lower cost structure. Therefore, the acquisition will require terminations of those executives who are associated with the redundant assets. In some cases, target company executives are key to efficiency creation, and their retention after the acquisition is critical to merger success. Likewise, when acquiring company executives possess superior resources and capabilities, termination of redundant target company executives is a key to acquisition success.

Table 7.2. Managerial Goals in Mergers and Acquisitions

Cluster	Objectives	Goals
1 Horizontal	Exploit economies of scale and scope	• Transfer acquirer's expertise into target company. • Create economies of scale by expanding capacity. • Acquire target company expertise.
2 Vertical	Reduce dependence on suppliers and buyers	• Exploit managerial expertise to reduce firm risk and costs. • Utilize interlocking qualities of target firm. • Reduce supplier risk and improve efficiencies.
3 Concentric	Expand product lines and markets	• Increase market share. • Diversify product lines. • Acquire target's marketing capacities. • Acquire target's distribution capacities. • Broaden firm's customer base. • Expand capacity.
4 Diversification	Enter new businesses	• Utilize surplus cash flow. • Reduce risk and cost of entering new industry. • Fulfill personal vision of acquirer's CEO.
5 Conglomerate	Maximize and utilize financial capabilities	• Promote visibility with investors. • Utilize financial strength of acquirer. • Decrease earnings cyclicality. • Divest assets of target company.

Source: Walter and Barney (1990).

In Cluster 2, acquisitions are used to either reduce risk and cost in value-chain relationships or improve the efficiency of value-chain transfers. In the latter case, a firm may acquirer a supplier that is squeezing the firm's profit margins by frequently raising prices. Firms may also acquire a supplier to guarantee the supply of components and decrease the risk of supply disruptions. In the latter case, a firm may acquire a supplier to integrate it with its production operations, in order to improve product functionality or reliability. For example, Caterpillar is a highly integrated manufacturer of earth-moving equipment, producing almost all components necessary to assemble its equipment in-house. Vertical integration increases costs; however, it also gives Caterpillar greater control over product functionality and reliability. Therefore, higher integration costs are more than offset by Caterpillar's ability to charge premium prices for the superior reliability and functionality of its equipment.

The goals listed in Cluster 3 emphasize expansion of the firm's existing products and markets. Diversification is not a goal in this objective category. Firms acquire other firms as a means of expanding their current product lines and markets, increasing market share and competitive position, and enhancing the ability to serve customers within their industry. Firms may be targeted for acquisition because they possess marketing and distribution capabilities that can help expand another firm's existing products into new markets. In such cases, target executives may play an important role in helping the acquirer establish a strong competitive position in the target firm's market.

Cluster 4 involves diversification into new products or industries. In many cases, firms use excess cash flow generated from a strong competitive position within their existing product line to acquire new businesses. In Cluster 5, firms make acquisitions for reasons other than to increase firm growth or to improve economic efficiencies. Instead, firms attempt to benefit by influencing their stock price or reducing earnings variability through diversification of their asset base.

In ranking different goals, Walter and Barney found that different goals were rated as more or less important within each objective category. For example, the most important goal in vertical acquisitions was to manage critical dependencies in the firm's value chain. In concentric acquisitions, the most important goal was to expand product lines. In conglomerate acquisitions, the most important goal was to utilize financial capabilities to enter new businesses. In horizontal acquisitions, however, several goals were rated as equally important: (a) to enter new businesses, (b) create economies of scale and scope efficiencies, (c) expand product lines, and (d) manage critical dependencies. This finding suggests that horizontal mergers are often driven by multiple goals and are designed to simultaneously achieve several objectives. It also suggests that firms making horizontal acquisitions are equally interested in increasing their market power as they are in improving efficiencies.

In conclusion, executives acquire firms for a multitude of reasons. Moreover, they often seek to achieve multiple objectives through an acquisition. This fact further adds to the complexity of using simple classification systems to categorize acquisitions. Because acquisitions may have multiple objectives, many acquisitions cannot easily be fit into a single category.

Strategic Drivers of Mergers and Acquisitions

Joseph Bower at Harvard's Graduate School of Business extended this line of thinking by considering the effects of industry structure, globalization, and rapid technological change in motivating M&As.[4] He argued that M&As occur for five reasons: (a) to eliminate overcapacity in a mature industry, (b) to expand geographically by acquiring smaller competitors in a fragmented industry, (c) to extend product lines and global coverage, (d) to acquire technologies in lieu of developing new technologies in-house, and (e) to establish a competitive position in an emerging industry. In evaluating each of these merger types, we begin to see how different M&A motivations create differing needs for target company executive resources and capabilities.

Growth and Survival of the Firm

As industries mature, the rate of growth begins to slow. To sustain historical rates of growth, competitors must compete more aggressively for existing customers. Competition is heightened in industries with high fixed-cost structures such as automobiles and steel. Because firms in mature industries have high break-even points, even small declines

Table 7.3. *Strategic Drivers of Mergers and Acquisitions*

#	M&A type	Strategy driver	Objectives
1	Overcapacity M&As	Mature industry	• Eliminate overcapacity in industry. • Increase market share. • Create more efficient operations.
2	Geographic rollups	Fragmented industry	• Expand geographically. • Operating units remain local.
3	Product and market extension M&As	Diversification globalization	• Extend products lines. • Extend global coverage.
4	M&As as R&D	Technological change	• Use acquisitions to acquire market position in lieu of in-house R&D.
5	Industry convergence	Emerging industries	• Establish a competitive position in an emerging industry.

Source: Bower (2001), pp. 93–101.

in sales can result in losses. As a means of survival, stronger firms will acquire weaker firms. The objective is to close less-competitive facilities, eliminate less-effective managers, and rationalize administrative processes. Successful acquisitions result in higher market share, more efficient operations, better managers, and lower industry capacity.

Bower discussed three strategic goals in overcapacity M&As: (a) rationalization of acquirer and target resources, (b) integration of organizational processes, and (c) assimilation of target firm value into the acquiring firm. Mergers between large, established firms in mature industries are often more difficult than other mergers because firms tend to be older and as a result have stronger corporate cultures and more deeply ingrained organizational processes and value systems. This situation makes it more difficult to assimilate the target's culture into the acquirer's culture, and is exacerbated when firms are relatively equal in size because the target is more likely to resist integration.

Acquisitions that are made to eliminate excess capacity are often "win–lose" transactions because they involve the closing of inefficient facilities and elimination of inefficient resources. Typically the target company's facilities and resources are the ones affected. In many cases, target company employees have little to gain. The result is interfirm power struggles and battles for control as target executives and employees fight to retain their positions. In many instances, the best executives from the target company—those who have the best outside opportunities—are the ones who depart. It may take time for target company employees to accept the acquisition. Moreover, it may take years for employees to learn the new organizational processes and values the acquiring firm imposes on them. Cultural differences often intensify over time as target company employees resist integration. As a result, overcapacity M&As have a high failure rate despite the significant potential for creating value.

The second merger type—geographic rollups—involves larger firms that expand geographically by acquiring smaller firms in local and regional markets. The acquirer builds economies of scale and scope efficiencies by spreading administrative costs such as purchasing, accounting, cash management, treasury, economic analysis, and strategic planning over a larger number of units. Acquiring companies can also increase market power when they acquire companies in markets where they currently have little presence. Target companies, in turn, benefit by using the acquirer's operating systems to lower their operating costs and to improve customer value.

Geographic rollups occur most frequently in fragmented industries composed of a large number of small businesses that serve local communities or regional markets. Examples of these businesses include financial services, insurance, and health care. Because customer relationships are so critical in these industries, it is important that the acquirer retain key target company executives, employees, and customers. Unlike overcapacity M&As, there is little rationalization of assets. Acquired units are often allowed to operate with little interference. The acquirer's objective is to help each acquired unit expand its resources and capabilities rather than to reduce or eliminate them. As a result, target company executives and employees are more likely to support the acquisition and to cooperate with the acquirer as it makes changes in the acquired unit's systems. Because many acquired companies may have unique processes and values—especially in family-run businesses—the acquirer can move more slowly making changes.

The third merger type—product extension mergers—are designed to extend the acquiring firm's product lines. The primary objective is to acquire businesses that operate in different product areas (i.e., diversification). Diversification is a means of expanding the firm's rate of growth, especially when the firm's existing products and services have begun to mature. In addition, it is a way to improve corporate-level profit by acquiring businesses that generate higher profit margins than the firm's existing product portfolio.

Diversification acquisitions create value in two ways. First, the acquirer shares value-chain activities across different businesses. This process creates economies of scale and scope efficiencies by leveraging corporate-level administrative costs across multiple businesses. Second, the acquirer transfers competencies between firms. Value transfer can occur in either direction—from the acquirer to the target, from the target to the acquirer, or both. In any case, the objective is to improve product functionality and performance of the acquirer, target, or both firms.

As in the case of overcapacity M&As, it is easier for large acquirers to integrate smaller targets. A merger of equals often leads to battles for corporate control, in which target company executives fight to retain their positions and resist attempts by the acquirer to change its existing systems, processes, values, and corporate culture. The target's executive team may or may not be receptive to integration efforts. On the one hand, retaining the target's executive team is often necessary when the acquirer buys businesses it does not understand well. In these cases, target executives play an important role helping the acquirer learn and absorb target-company knowledge. On the other hand, target-company executives who resist integration can destroy the acquiring firm's efforts to integrate the target company. In such cases, it is important to identify these executives and replace them—the sooner, the better.

The Effect of Globalization and Technology Trends

Three other merger types—market extension, M&As as research and development (R&D), and industry convergence M&As—are a product of strong globalization and technology trends during the last 30 years. Market extension mergers extend the acquirer's geographic reach, especially globally. Both globalization and technology trends have spurred cross-border M&As. Advancements in communications and transportation have made it easier for firms to enter foreign markets. In addition, The costs of R&D have risen and product life cycles have become shorter in a wide range of industries, including telecommunications, computers, semiconductors, electronics, and pharmaceuticals. Firms in globalizing industries have been forced to expand abroad in search of greater sales, in order to recover the rising costs of R&D and new product development.

Multinational firms transfer knowledge, resources, and capabilities among subsidiaries in order to lower costs, improve product functionality and reliability, and increase decision-making effectiveness. Successfully integrating a firm that is located abroad, however, is generally more difficult than integrating a domestic firm. When firms compete in foreign markets, they operate with a "liability of foreignness." Physical distance makes communications and face-to-face interactions more difficult. In addition, the firm is faced with language, cultural, legal, and political barriers that make decision making more difficult.

In cross-border acquisitions, acquirers need to rely on both their own executives and executives in the acquired company as an indispensible tool for successfully integrating and operating an acquired foreign unit. On the one hand, the acquiring company's own executives are an instrumental tool for transferring the company's policies and procedures into the foreign subsidiary. Many industries such as automobiles, computers, semiconductors, pharmaceuticals, and telecommunications have developed global industry structures. Value-chain activities, products, and distribution channels have become largely standardized, which provides firms with opportunities to lower costs through product standardization and economies of scale. In such cases, acquirers can generally use their own executives to transfer standardized policies and procedures across units worldwide.

On the other hand, target company executives can play an important role helping acquiring firms overcome cultural, language, political, and legal barriers that might otherwise hinder communications, negatively affect decision-making effectiveness, and make integration difficult. Many industries such as food, beverages, and consumer products have localized value chains. Firms must customize products and services and respond to the local market's unique distribution, sales channel, and customer service needs. In these cases, retention of local executives is critical in that it helps the acquirer maintain a high level of local responsiveness to local customer needs.

A variety of companies have turned to acquisitions in lieu of in-house R&D as a means of acquiring new technologies. A good example is the pharmaceutical industry, which has recently experienced a number of megamergers by large players attempting to find new products to replace expiring patents (see Table 7.4). Pfizer, for example, announced the acquisition of Wyeth for $68 billion in January 2006. Pfizer's primary objective was to gain control of Wyeth's vaccines and biologic drugs. It expects these new drugs to help fill the void left by the expiration of its patent on Lipitor, its leading anticholesterol drug. The Pfizer-Wyeth merger came on the heals of Merck & Co.'s announcement that it would acquire Schering-Plough Corp. for $41.1 billion and Roche Holding AG's announcement that it would acquire Genentech for $47 billion. Merck gained control of the cardiovascular business of Schering-Plough, as well as its anti-inflammatory drug, Remicade. Roche and Genentech have a history of partnering, with Roche's three best-selling drugs coming from Genentech (Avastin, Herceptin, and Rituxan).

In some cases, M&As are an effective strategy for acquiring resources and capabilities faster than they could be developed in-house—and, presumably, at lower cost. Because this type of acquisition is designed to acquire the target company's resources and capabilities in R&D and product development, a critical goal is to retain the target's human resources. Acquiring firms, however, often approach M&A deals from a cost-cutting perspective. Pfizer, for example, acquired Warner-Lambert

Table 7.4. Largest Pharmaceutical Mergers: 2006–2009

	Date	Acquirer	Target	Value ($ Billion)
1	2009	Pfizer	Wyeth	68.0
2	2009	Roche Holding AG	Genentech	46.7
3	2006	Johnson & Johnson	Pfizer (Consumer Business)	16.6
4	2007	AstraZeneca PLC	MedImmune	14.6
5	2008	Teva Pharmaceutical	Barr Pharmaceuticals	8.8
6	2006	Teva Pharmaceutical	IVAX Corp.	7.4
7	2008	Eli Lilly & Co.	ImClone Systems	6.5
8	2006	Novartis AG	Chiron Corp.	6.2
9	2006	Abbott Laboratories	Boston Scientific (Guidant Intervention Business)	4.6
10	2006	Abbott Laboratories	Kos Pharmaceuticals	4.1

Source: Thomson Reuters, SDC Database.

in 2000 for $90 billion. Its primary goal was to gain control of Lipitor. In 2002, Pfizer acquired Pharmacia for $60 billion. Its primary goal was to gain control of Celebrex, Pharmacia's pain-relief drug. In both cases, Pfizer followed with massive cost cutting, executive terminations, and employee layoffs. Despite the acquisition of these popular drugs, Pfizer's stock price has fallen 69% since May 2000.

The last merger type—the "industry convergent M&A"—is a product of rapid globalization and evolving technology trends. Industry boundaries are in a constant state of change. New technologies such as the Internet have created new industries such as online retailing. Globalization has resulted in large multinational firms that can leverage superior resources and capabilities across multiple businesses and markets to both increase their market power and extend the boundaries of their industries. Some attempts to extend the boundaries of the firm fail, such as Sears Roebuck and Company's attempt to combine its retailing business with the brokerage business of Dean Witter Reynolds in 1981. Other attempts to extend the boundaries of the firm succeed, such as the merger between Dean Witter Reynolds and Morgan Stanley Group to create a large, diversified financial services firm in 1997. If globalization and technology trends continue, M&As that are designed to create new industries or extend the boundaries of a firm's existing industry should become increasingly common.

In sum, not all M&As are the same. Each merger type is driven by a unique set of objectives. Moreover, acquisitions are often used to achieve multiple goals that cut across two or more merger categories. Globalization and the rapid evolution of technology are creating new opportunities for firms to use M&As to extend the boundaries of the firm, expand geographically, diversify into new businesses, and improve profitability. The decision to retain or replace target-company executives is not an easy one. In many acquisitions, retention of target-company executives may be a key determinant of acquisition success or failure. In other acquisitions, terminating redundant executives, or executives who resist integration efforts, may be an equally important determinant of synergy creation and long-term performance. An in-depth understanding of merger motivations and objectives is an important first step in identifying the needs of the acquisition and the role that the target company's top management team may or may not play in achieving the acquirer's objectives.

CHAPTER 8

After the Merger: Why Executives Stay or Leave

We were "metamorphosed" from a publicly traded U.S. Fortune 500 company to the U.S. subsidiary of a Swedish multinational. The elimination of major departments and location issues had to be addressed at an early stage and continued to be a problem long after the acquisition.

I had a close personal and professional relationship with my counterpart in the new parent company. I admired the Swedish global management style. They gave us greatly expanded professional responsibilities in the M&A area but also gave us a lot of professional independence.

—Top executive who stayed after his company was acquired by a Swedish multinational

Strategic Versus Organizational Fit

Mergers and acquisitions (M&As) is a broad field. It is often split into "hard" versus "soft" issues. The "hard side" of M&As deals with quantitative issues such as net present value analysis, strategic fit analysis, stock price measurements following the merger announcement, and securities law.[1] These issues are generally the domain of accountants, financial analysts, and corporate attorneys. The "soft side" of M&As deals with qualitative issues such as postmerger integration, strategy formulation and execution, and executive leadership.[2] These issues are generally the domain of the organization's top executives. This includes the firm's divisional executive heads and the executive heads of the firm's staff functions such as strategic planning and human resource management.

We can also view M&As using a pre- versus postmerger perspective. During the premerger period, strategic fit issues prevail. Analysts are preoccupied with analyzing potential synergies and sources of value creation in a proposed merger. In addition, firms focus on estimating future cash flows and financial returns and negotiating a purchase price that does not capitalize future cash flows from the merger. During the postmerger period, organizational fit issues prevail. Executives focus on how to effectively integrate the resources and systems of the two merging firms. The objective is to exploit scale and scope synergies. In addition, executives focus on transferring capabilities between firms. Here the objective is to improve product performance and reliability, increase decision-making effectiveness, and enhance long-term performance.

David Jemison (University of Texas at Austin) and Sim Sitkin (Duke University) defined organizational fit as the "match between administrative practices, cultural practices, and personnel characteristics of the target and parent firms."[3] Acquiring companies typically spend a great deal of time analyzing strategic fit issues during the negotiation process. Strategic fit—the source of synergy creation—is often the primary basis for determining a purchase price. In contrast, organizational fit issues are often ignored until the acquisition has already taken place. However, organizational fit affects how firms are integrated and how executives and employees from the two merging firms work together on a day-to-day basis. Not only does poor organizational fit increase the costs of integration, but it can also derail it.

The way in which the target company's top management team is managed after the acquisition is a critical part of the integration process. Executives play an instrumental role in defining the firm's mission, determining strategic objectives, formulating and executing strategy, and evaluating organizational performance. Following an acquisition, they play an important role helping the acquiring company integrate the cultures, systems, and values of the two companies. In addition, they can play an important role communicating with employees and keeping employees informed about the objectives of the merger and how the merger will affect their future roles in the organization. In doing so, executives' actions can help minimize the negative effects of the merger on employee uncertainty, commitment to the organization, and productivity.

Why Executives Stay or Leave

Individual Characteristics and Motivations of Executives

I have interviewed several hundred target company executives following their firm's acquisition. About one-third of the executives I interviewed reported that they left the company for reasons that had little to do with the acquisition (e.g., to take advantage of a better career opportunity or for family reasons). Another one-third reported that they were terminated. They were replaced by an executive from the acquiring firm, their position was eliminated, or they were forced to leave when an entire division was eliminated. Another one-third reported that they left to avoid termination, because their job status was reduced, or because they felt alienated from executives in the acquiring firm. In many cases, these executives were made to feel that they were no longer a valued member of the firm's executive team. In almost all cases, these executives reported that they would not have left their firm had it not been acquired. Figure 8.1 shows a partial list of the many comments made to me by target company executives regarding their impressions of the acquiring firm.

Companies can expect to lose an average of 8%–10% of their executives each year through normal attrition. In the first year following acquisition, companies can expect to lose about three times this amount—about one-quarter of the target's executive team can be expected to depart. A large portion of the higher turnover that occurs after an acquisition is involuntary. Either the executive is terminated or he or she leaves to avoid termination, reduced status, or a hostile work environment. Individual characteristics are an important determinant of how executives react during the post-merger integration process. Some executives have a greater tolerance for uncertainty and ambiguity than others. Other executives are superior strategic thinkers or have superior capabilities managing complex organizations. Therefore, certain types of executives are more likely to leave than other executives when they are subjected to the same organizational events.

❖ "The acquirer didn't understand our business."
❖ "They had no interest in our local community."
❖ "They didn't care about our employees."
❖ "They stressed conformity over performance."
❖ "They had a 'not made here, no damn good' mentality."
❖ "They didn't honor their promises . . . unethical and dishonest."
❖ "They took my division away from me."
❖ "They gave me a job with lower job title and fewer responsibilities."
❖ "If I had not left, I would have been terminated."

Figure 8.1. Why executives left after the acquisition

For example, older, more senior executives are more likely to depart more quickly than younger, less senior executives. Walsh found that close to 40% of target company chairs, chief executive officers, and presidents depart within 5 years after an acquisition.[4] Significantly fewer—about 27%—of target company vice presidents, controllers, secretaries, and treasurers leave during the same period. Acquiring firms are more likely to replace an acquired company's top executives with their own executives to symbolically demonstrate that they are in charge. In addition, an acquiring firm is able to more effectively control the integration process and execute strategic change when its own executives occupy the top positions. More senior target company executives may also be more likely to leave voluntarily. They are more accustomed to being in charge than less senior executives. Consequently, they may prefer to depart rather than having to report to executives in the acquiring firm. Other executives may use the acquisition as an opportunity to retire.

Donald Hambrick (The Pennsylvania State University) and Bert Cannella (Tulane University) analyzed the effect of status as a cause of an executive's decision to leave after an acquisition.[5] They argued that acquisitions disrupt social standings.[6] In many cases, acquisitions lead to lower job status for executives. Acquirers feel superior and make acquired company executives feel inferior. Target company executives lose status and autonomy and feel alienated. These conditions motivate executives to leave. Other acquisitions lead to greater status for executives. Acquirers value their contributions and make their feelings known. This enhances the positive feelings of executives about the merger and motivates them to stay.

Hambrick and Cannella drew heavily from the concept of relative standing developed by Robert Frank in his book *Choosing the Right Pond: Human Behavior and the Quest for Status*.[7] Frank describes relative standing as an individual's status relative to others in a social setting. In most social settings, some hold positions of greater status than others. Those with lower status only stay if they are compensated in other ways, such as through greater monetary compensation or a sense of belonging and acceptance. A good example is Lance Armstrong's record-breaking seven consecutive wins in the Tour de France from 1999 to 2005. Armstrong's singular goal was to win the Tour de France each year. His ability to win the Tour de France depended heavily on the willingness of his teammates ("domestiques") to support him during the race (e.g., by shielding him from the wind, passing water to him, and supporting him during sprints). His teammates sacrificed status by not competing to win in the Tour de France. In return, they received bonuses. In addition, Armstrong acted as their domestique to help them win other cycling events throughout the year.

When executives—who are accustomed to status and recognition in their own firms—are given positions of authority and status, receive greater compensation, and are shown respect by the acquiring firm's executives, they are more likely to stay. When not, they are more likely to leave.

Figure 8.2 outlines the different reasons why executives stay or leave following a merger or acquisition. Four factors influence the probability of a target executive's decision to stay or leave: (a) the individual characteristics of executives, (b) attributes of the merger, (c) cross-border M&As, (d) firm characteristics, and (e) structure of the target firm's industry. For example, individual characteristics of the executives themselves tend to motivate executives to stay or leave. Older, more senior executives are more likely to leave. Executives who are given status and autonomy in the postmerger firm are more likely to stay.

(1) Executive characteristics
❖ Age (-)
❖ Seniority (-)
❖ Status (+)
❖ Autonomy (+)

(2) Merger characteristics
❖ Hostile negotiations (-)
❖ Contested tender offers (-)
❖ Multiple bidders (-)

(3) Cross-border mergers & acquisitions
❖ Foreign multinational (-)
❖ Cultural differences (-)
❖ Acquisition experience of acquirer (-)
❖ International experience of foreign acquirer (+)

(4) Target company characteristics
❖ Size differences (-)
❖ Poor premerger performance (-)

(5) Industry characteristics
❖ Global industry (-)

- Executives more likely to leave
+ Executives more likely to stay

Figure 8.2. What determines why executives stay or leave?

Merger Characteristics

Feelings of status are developed early in the acquisition negotiation process. Negotiations that are conducted in a professional atmosphere and promote feelings of equality and mutual respect tend to create positive feelings about the merger between both parties. This promotes executive retention after the transaction is completed.[8] Walsh examined a wide range of merger characteristics to determine whether they influenced postmerger executive retention. The variables included

1. hostile negotiations;
2. tender offers;
3. multiple bidders;
4. number of counter-offers made before an agreement was reached;
5. time taken to negotiate an agreement;
6. method of payment (i.e., stock, cash, or combination);
7. premium paid for the target; and
8. public assurance that the target's executive team would be retained.

Hostile negotiations were the only merger characteristic that was associated with high turnover during the first year after the acquisition. Hostility openly expressed during the acquisition negotiation stage clearly creates negative feelings that motivate target executives to leave quickly after the transaction. However, few acquisitions—5% or less—are openly hostile.[9] Walsh found that tender offers were associated with higher target executive turnover in the second year after the acquisition. Tender offers are offers to buy a company that are made directly to shareholders. In hostile acquisitions, potential buyers intentionally bypass the target's top management team, since it opposes the acquisition. In other cases, a potential buyer is likely to negotiate an agreement with target company management before extending a formal tender offer to shareholders.

Therefore, not all tender offers are hostile. Hambrick and Cannella found a strong relationship between contested (i.e., hostile) tender offers and target company executive turnover beginning in the first month and continuing through the second year after the acquisition. Uncontested tender offers did not promote executive departures. In short, a negotiation process that is characterized by a hostile climate can have pervasive effects on the perceptions of target company executives. Many are likely to leave. For acquiring companies, retaining target company executives after the acquisition may also create the possibility that target executives will openly oppose organizational changes and hinder integration efforts. In such cases, it is best if acquiring companies replace these executives soon after the acquisition is completed.

In addition to hostile negotiations and contested tender offers, target company executive turnover tends to be higher when the target company is subjected to takeover interest from multiple bidders. The market apparently recognizes inefficiencies in firms that results in lower stock prices. This attracts multiple bidders. In cases where inefficient management exists, acquiring firms are unlikely to retain target executives once the firm is acquired.

A final finding is worth noting. Public assurances made by the acquiring firm during merger negotiations that it will retain target company executives after the acquisition appear to be hollow. There is no substantiated relationship between public assurances of executive retention and actual retention after the acquisition. It appears as though such assurances should be taken with a grain of salt by executives considering the sale of their company.

Walsh concluded that merger characteristics in general fall short of explaining a large portion of the very high level of turnover that occurs in target companies following an acquisition. Hostile negotiations and contested tender offers are the two strongest indicators. However, his findings did suggest that acquisitions have strong effects that continue to be felt 4 or 5 years after the transaction has been completed.

Cross-Border Mergers and Acquisitions

Much of my own research has focused on the differences between foreign and domestic M&As.[10] My findings suggest that the turnover effects of acquisitions are intensified in cross-border transactions. That is, executives depart at higher rates over time in firms that are acquired by a foreign multinational. The primary difference between foreign and domestic M&As is in the timing of turnover. In domestic acquisitions, turnover occurs more quickly—primarily in the first 2 years after the acquisition. In cross-border acquisitions, the full effects of the acquisition continue to be felt for 5 to

6 years after the acquisition. In general, domestic acquirers are faced with fewer cultural differences as they attempt to integrate the target company. In addition, acquiring a company that is physically closer creates fewer travel and communications barriers. In cross-border acquisitions, foreign acquirers are faced with integrating a target company that is not only physically more distant but is also culturally different. These factors appear to cause foreign acquirers to move more slowly in making strategic and organizational changes in the firms they acquire internationally.

Target company executives tend to depart more quickly when the acquiring firm has already made acquisitions in their country.[11] Acquiring firms accumulate integration experience through past acquisitions and this experience gives them more confidence in subsequent acquisitions. As they develop acquisition capabilities, they also feel more comfortable integrating future acquired firms using their own executives. Moreover, experience investing in the same countries allows companies to develop knowledge that enables them to more efficiently manage culture differences in future acquisitions. As the foreign firm makes additional foreign investments in the same country, it becomes less dependent on the target company for local knowledge. Consequently, foreign acquirers are more likely to use their own executives to integrate firms when they have acquisition experience. They also become more adept at managing cultural differences, which may increase the desire of some target executives to stay.

Firm Characteristics

Do characteristics of the parent or target company influence the tendency of target executives to stay or leave? One factor that appears to decrease target executive retention is large size differences between merging firms.[12] When the acquirer is large relative to the acquired firm, it is more likely that the acquirer has a supply of skilled executives who can be transferred into the acquired firm. Moreover, executives in small target companies may be less able to manage executive positions in larger, more complex, and more bureaucratic acquiring firms. Psychological barriers may also lead to greater turnover. Target executives are accustomed to status, autonomy, and a high level of managerial discretion. When acquired by a larger firm, many target executives are more likely to feel like a small fish in a big pond—they feel a sense of lost status and autonomy that causes them to consider leaving. If the target is equal in size to the acquirer, target executives are more likely to feel comfortable with the transition to the acquiring firm's structure and systems.

Firm performance is also an important determinant of turnover in acquired companies. Two questions relate to the target company's pre-merger performance:

1. Does poor target company performance lead to higher executive turnover after acquisition?
2. Is poor target company performance a primary motivation of M&A activity?

The answer to the first question is yes. Poor premerger performance is a good indicator that target executives will lose their jobs after an acquisition. Cannella and Hambrick found that poor performance was associated with higher target executive turnover up to 4 years after the acquisition.[13] Performance is often attributed to a firm's executive team. When the firm performs well relative to competitors, executives are viewed as competent. When the firm performs poorly, executives are viewed as less competent. Therefore, acquiring firms typically have greater confidence in target company executives if their company performed well before the acquisition. These executives are more likely to be retained. In poorly performing target firms, it is more likely that the acquirer will replace executives with its own.

The answer to the second question is no. Research by Walsh and Kosnik found that poorly performing target companies are more likely to become the subject of takeover interest by corporate raiders.[14] Well-known corporate raiders include Robert Bass, the Belzberg family, Asher Edelman, Sir James Goldsmith, Carl Icahn, Irwin Jacobs, Kirk Kerkorian, Carl Lindner, David Murdock, Nelson Peltz, T. Boone Pickens, Victor Posner, Saul Steinberg, and Harold Clark Simmons. When a corporate raider acquires a poorly performing target company, the motivation is often to rid the target company of inefficient management, install new management to improve firm performance, and generate profits by later selling the firm.

The notion that incompetent or inefficient managers become the subject of takeover interest is commonly called the "market for corporate control." An assumption is that executives sometimes engage in behavior that maximizes their own interests at the expense of shareholders. Executives may engage in activities that represent conflicts of interest in three areas: (a) effort, (b) risk, and (c) time horizons.[15] For example, executives may invest in low-risk projects to minimize work effort, free up time for leisure activities, and increase employment stability. In other instances, executives may invest in high-risk projects that maximize opportunities for future wealth creation and promotion. Lastly, executives may engage in activities that maximize short-term performance at the expense of long-term performance. In each case, the risk-return relationship preferred by shareholders is violated by executives' actions.

Agency theory describes the relationship between shareholders, the firms' board of directors, and executives. The owners of the firm—shareholders—elect a board of directors to look after their interests. The board is responsible for hiring a chief executive, monitoring firm performance, and taking corrective action when firm performance falters or executives pursue activities that are inconsistent with the interests of shareholders. In many cases, boards fail to intervene to correct for poor performance or corrupt behavior on the part of executives. In such cases, acquisitions represent an effective remedy for the breakdown of agency relationships. Outside firms bid on poor performing firms, replace incompetent management, and restore firm performance. In this sense, M&As are thought to reflect a "market for corporate control," wherein outside firms step in to buy target firms when boards fail to act appropriately.[16]

Research, however, shows that most target companies outperform the market and perform well relative to industry competitors prior to their acquisition.[17] This suggests that most target companies are acquired because acquirers see potential value in the acquisition. That is, they acquire the target to grow sales and improve corporate performance. In addition, there is little evidence that target company executives "entrench" themselves by engaging in activities that increase their continued tenure.[18] In reality, many target companies have premerger turnover rates that are higher than in other companies. In sum, there is little evidence to suggest that the "market for corporate control" is a primary driver of most

M&As. While some acquisitions are motivated by poor performance, the majority of acquisitions are driven by the desire of acquiring firms to buy good performers—companies with assets, skills, and executive competencies that can help them increase their own performance.

Industry Characteristics

Do industry characteristics influence the retention of a target company's top management team? Studies have focused on the concept of "relatedness." Two conditions typically define whether two companies are related: (a) firms sell products and services to the same customers, and (b) firms use the same resources, capabilities, and value-chain activities (e.g., production processes) to make the product or service.[19] When firms possess common value-chain activities or use the same distribution channels, there is often the potential for creating synergies by sharing common activities. By sharing common activities, redundant assets can be eliminated and resources consolidated. In doing so, costs are lowered by spreading costs over a greater number of units sold. When firms are unrelated, no such commonalities exist. In such cases, acquirers are like portfolio investors in that they take ownership of the firm but are likely to allow the firm to operate autonomously, since few opportunities to create synergies exist.

Stock market movements support this logic. Stock prices of both acquiring and target firms tend to increase significantly on the day of an acquisition announcement.[20] The significant increase in stock prices suggests that shareholders expect the acquisition to produce synergies and create value. There is little evidence, however, that acquisitions actually deliver expected synergies. In reality, about one-half of all acquiring firms experience declines in accounting performance (e.g., return on sales, return on equity, and return on assets) following an acquisition. A large number of studies have concluded that "related" mergers do not perform any better than "unrelated" mergers.[21] Thus, relatedness is considered to be a desirable condition for merger success, but it does not guarantee it. One reason that relatedness may not be a good indicator of future merger success is that many acquiring firms fail to successfully integrate the entities they acquire. Moreover, there is a wide variation in the degree of integration that exists across different mergers.[22] In the absence of effective integration, value creation is impossible, regardless of the potential synergies that may exist.[23]

One might expect that greater relatedness between merging firms would also lead to greater executive turnover in acquired firms. If merging firms are able to successfully combine value-chain activities, they should be able to eliminate asset redundancies and successfully operate the newly merged firm using fewer resources. As assets are reduced or eliminated, acquiring firms may find it desirable to also reduce the target's executive resources. Acquiring firms may also feel more comfortable operating the acquired firm using their own executives when operating processes are similar. Therefore, highly related merging firms should be associated with higher target company executive turnover.

Studies have found few significant relationships between relatedness and postmerger executive turnover. Walsh's research found little relationship between relatedness and executive turnover across the different Federal Trade Commission categories (i.e., horizontal, vertical, product extension, market extension, and unrelated).[24] Cannella and Hambrick tested the effect of relatedness on executive turnover using "expert judges," who categorized the relatedness of different acquisitions based on descriptions of the merging firms' businesses.[25] They also found few significant relationships. Their single finding was that unrelated acquisitions experienced greater turnover in the first month after the acquisition. This was contrary to expectations. One possibility for this finding is that unrelated firms have greater cultural gaps. These cultural gaps result in communications problems during the negotiation process that motivate some target executives to leave. Overall, however, relatedness appears to be a weak predictor of executive turnover in acquired companies.

My own research has focused on analyzing the effect of an industry's global structure when a firm is acquired by a foreign multinational firm.[26] I utilized the concept of "transnational integration" (TI) developed by Stephen Kobrin of the Wharton School of Business at the University of Pennsylvania.[27] Global firms benefit by integrating their activities across national borders. For example, they standardize products and services. They centralize research and development, purchasing, cash flow management, accounting, and other functional activities. They consolidate manufacturing in large-scale facilities in order to lower costs through economies of scale and scope. They coordinate the shipment of components from highly specialized plants located throughout the world to regional assembly plants. From there, the assembled product can be transported to the end user. Integration leads to lower costs and higher product reliability. Therefore, domestic firms often find it difficult to match the cost and reliability advantages of globally integrated firms.

Kobrin measured a firm's global structure by calculating the portion of a firm's international sales that are intrafirm. Some industries are more likely to benefit from global integration than others. On the one hand, food and beverages are difficult to standardize because of strong differences in local preferences from country to country. Dairy products are difficult to consolidate globally because they are highly perishable and expensive to transport. Therefore, competition tends to be dominated by domestic competitors that serve local customers. These industries don't often benefit from global integration. Figure 8.3 shows a list of local versus global industries from Kobrin's research.

On the other hand, computers and semiconductors are cheap to transport and can be stored for long periods without deterioration. Thus, they can be produced in large-scale plants located in low-wage countries

Local industries	Global industries
• Paper boxes.	• Motor vehicles.
• Leather products.	• Communications equipment.
• Ferrous metals.	• Electronic components.
• Fabricated metals.	• Computers.
• Preserved fruits and vegetables.	• Farm machinery.
• Dairy products.	• Photographic equipment.
• Grain mill products.	• Engines.
• Machinery.	• Scientific measuring instruments.
• Food products.	• Optical goods.
• Forgings.	• Industrial chemicals.
• Plumbing.	• Metalworking machines.
• Pulp and paper.	• Nonferrous metals.
• Household appliances.	• Apparel.
	• Screw machine products.

Figure 8.3. Global Industry Structure

Source: Kobrin (1991), p. 22.

in order to lower costs. Once produced, they can be transported at low cost to consumers worldwide. Because consumers like the same products, research and development (R&D) can be centralized and products standardized. These industries benefit greatly from global integration. In global industries, plants are highly specialized. Subsidiaries in each country tend to specialize in the production of a single component. This increases scale and scope efficiencies. Components are then moved from subsidiaries to assembly plants located near the final consumer. By assembling products close to the end user, transportation costs can be minimized. Therefore, global industries are characterized by a high portion of international sales being made within the firm—from one subsidiary to another.

My research found that executives in target companies that compete in global industries tend to depart more quickly than executives in target companies that compete in local industries. The effect of global integration leads to higher executive turnover immediately after the acquisition. This effect continues up to 6 years after the acquisition. Therefore, the effects of competing in a global industry are immediate and long-term. In global industries, local knowledge is less critical to a firm's success. A firm's success follows from selling a standardized product worldwide. Cultural differences are minimal because consumers desire the same standardized product. Retaining local managers is not a high priority in cross-border acquisitions in global industries. For the global firm, it is important to transfer its own standardized technologies and organizational processes into the acquired firm in order to integrate the target's operations with its other worldwide subsidiaries. The global firm's own executives are an important means for transferring the firm's strategy abroad.

CHAPTER 9

Conclusion

The new owners are young, aggressive, informal, and visionary—a complete contrast to our former owners. They are also risk takers and have made large investments in our people and facilities—in contrast to our former owners, who didn't believe in cross-fertilization at the top, middle, or lower levels of management. The new owners are quite the opposite and have good results to show for it.

—Top executive who stayed with his division after it
was sold by his parent company to another firm

Categorizing Executive Turnover

There is now an abundance of evidence to show that mergers and acquisitions can be tumultuous for executives. Acquiring firms must be prepared to lose about one-quarter of the target company's top management team in the first year following an acquisition. They should expect an additional 15% to leave in the second year. That means that acquiring companies can expect to lose about 40% of an acquired company's top management team during the 2 years after the acquisition.

If the departure of target company executives after the acquisition were associated with higher postmerger performance, then there would be little need for acquiring firms to be concerned with high postmerger executive turnover rates. However, my research shows that the relationship between executive turnover and postmerger performance is a complex one. In some acquisitions, executive turnover may benefit the acquirer by replacing poor performers, reducing resistance to the acquisition, and eliminating redundant executive resources. In other acquisitions, executive turnover may be detrimental to postmerger performance, such as when a primary objective of the acquisition is to acquire target company executive knowledge and capabilities.

Acquiring firms should not approach an acquisition with a simple notion about whether executive turnover is good or bad. They need to first develop a firm grasp of acquisition motivations and objectives before they assess executive leadership needs. Once the acquirer understands precisely what value it intends to create through an acquisition, it can then begin to match target executives to roles that support value creation and are compatible with acquisition objectives.

Voluntary Versus Involuntary Executive Turnover

Early research on turnover simply categorized turnover as "voluntary" or "involuntary."[1] Consider Figure 9.1. The target executive's decision to stay or leave after acquisition is determined by his or her perceptions of the positive and negative consequences of the acquisition for his or her career (Y axis) and the acquiring firm's perception of the executive (X axis). If the acquirer values the executive, and the executive views the acquisition favorably, he or she is likely to stay (Cell A). If the acquirer has a negative view of the executive, it is more likely to replace him or her (Cell B). In this case, it is assumed that the executive would like to stay; otherwise, he or she would have left. Alternatively, if the executive views the acquisition negatively, he or she may quit. In this case, the acquirer may or may not have a positive view of the executive. The executive leaves regardless of the acquirer's perceptions.

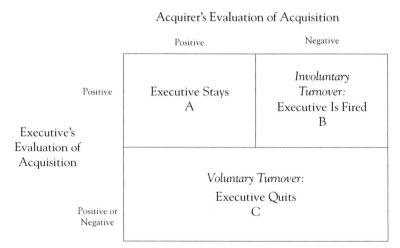

Figure 9.1. Voluntary versus involuntary turnover

Source: Adapted from Dalton, Tudor, and Krackhardt (1982).

Functional Versus Dysfunctional Executive Turnover

Viewing the executive's decision to leave as simply voluntary or involuntary, however, doesn't give us any information about whether the executive's departure affects the acquired company's performance after the acquisition. In Figure 9.2, Cell C from Figure 9.1 is divided into two cells based on whether the acquiring company views the executive's departure as beneficial or detrimental. In Cell D, the executive views staying as negative; therefore, he or she leaves. However, the acquirer views the executive's performance as poor and isn't concerned with the executive's departure. In Cell C, the executive is unhappy and decides to leave. Nevertheless, the acquirer values this executive. The executive's departure would clearly be dysfunctional in that it would negatively affect performance. For acquiring firms, viewing executive turnover in this manner is beneficial in two ways. First, it shows that acquiring firms that uniformly promote the retention of all target company executives end up wasting resources and efforts on retaining executives who add little value to the postmerger organization (executives in Cell D). Second, it suggests that acquiring firms need to focus on identifying executives who fall into Cell C. The departure of these executives would clearly be detrimental to the postmerger performance of the combined firm.

Acquirer's Evaluation of Acquisition

	Positive	Negative
Positive	Executive Stays A	*Beneficial Turnover:* Executive Is Fired B
Positive or Negative	*Detrimental Turnover:* Executive Quits C	*Beneficial Turnover:* Executive Quits D

Executive's Evaluation of Acquisition

Figure 9.2. Is executive turnover beneficial?

Source: Adapted from Dalton, Tudor, and Krackhardt (1982).

Avoidable Versus Unavoidable Executive Turnover

Firms should also consider whether an executive's decision to quit is unavoidable. Consider an acquiring firm that elevates a target company executive to a higher position with greater status, responsibilities, and compensation, only to have the executive depart soon thereafter. Executives leave for a wide range of reasons that have little to do with the acquisition. Some executives leave for family reasons (e.g., to move closer to family or to follow a spouse to a new job). Other executives leave because of health reasons. It wouldn't be profitable for firms to spend resources and time courting these executives. They will leave in any case.

This situation is reflected in Figure 9.3. Examples of turnover motivation in each category are reflected in Figure 9.4.[2] Cells C and D from Figure 9.2 are divided into separate groups based on whether the acquirer is able to influence the executive's decision to leave. For example, executives in Cell E may or may not view the acquisition favorably and leave the company for reasons that have little to do with the acquisition—for example, for personal reasons. The acquiring firm values this executive and would like him or her to stay; however, the acquirer can do little to keep the executive from leaving. Efforts to retain this executive would

Acquirer's Evaluation of Acquisition

		Positive	Negative
	Positive	Executive Stays A	Executive Is Fired B
Executive's Evaluation of Acquisition	Positive or Negative	*Detrimental* AND *Avoidable* Executive Quits C	*Avoidable* but *Beneficial* Executive Quits D
	Positive or Negative	*Detrimental* BUT *Unavoidable* Executive Quits E	*Unavoidable* but *Beneficial* Executive Quits F

Figure 9.3. Is executive turnover avoidable?

Source: Adapted from Abelson (1987).

Acquirer's Evaluation of Acquisition

		Positive	Negative
Executive's Evaluation of Acquisition	Positive	Executive Stays A	Executive Is Fired B • Poor Performance
	Positive or Negative	Executive Quits C • Higher Status • Higher Salary • Power	Executive Quits D • Low Status • Lost Autonomy • Cultural Conflict
	Positive or Negative	Executive Quits E • Family Reasons • Spouse	Executive Quits F • Retirement • Health

Figure 9.4. Reasons why executives depart

Source: Campion (1991).

likely be unsuccessful. Executives in Cell F also leave for reasons that have little to do with the acquisition—for example, to retire or because of health problems. In these cases, the acquiring firm is unconcerned with the executive's departure. It makes little sense for the acquirer to spend time and money encouraging these executives to stay.

Executives in Cells C and D have a positive view of the acquisition and prefer to stay. Therefore, any turnover of executives in Cells C and D—unlike executives in Cells E and F—is potentially avoidable. Executives in Cell D quit because they are unhappy with aspects of their job. For example, the executive may be unhappy with his or her job status following the acquisition and chooses to depart. Presumably, the loss of status reflects the acquiring company's perception of the executive—it views the executive negatively and is not unhappy to see him or her leave. Executives in Cell C, however, are viewed favorably. The acquiring company believes these executives can play important roles in the postmerger firm. Therefore, they would rather these executives not leave. However, these executives may leave anyway if they are presented with outside opportunities with other firms that offer greater compensation, status, responsibilities, and autonomy. Acquiring firms need to take prompt action to make sure that these executives do not leave.

Developing a Strategy for Managing Target Company Executives After the Acquisition

In sum, applying a simple strategy for managing an acquired company's top management team is likely to fail. On the one hand, an integration strategy that treats the acquired company's executive team as a single unit that needs to be replaced is like throwing the baby out with the bath water. You may eliminate bad performers, but you may also lose key executives who are crucial to the integration process. On the other hand, following a strategy that uniformly promotes the retention of the entire target company top management is costly and ineffective. It unnecessarily focuses management time and resources on executives whose departure would actually benefit the firm (e.g., bad performers) or whose departure is unavoidable (e.g., executives who leave for health reasons).

Step 1: Identifying Poor Performers

Poor performers should be replaced. These executives fall into cells B and D in Figure 9.5. Figure 9.5 implies that acquiring firms terminate executives in Cell B but not executives in Cell D. However, both sets of executives are valued poorly. Consider the highly publicized merger between Chrysler Corporation and Daimler-Benz in 1998. Within 2 years following the merger, most executives on Chrysler's top management team had resigned. Statements made to the national press suggested that most of Chrysler's executives left to avoid termination or demotion. Many Chrysler executives had spent much of their professional lives at Chrysler and had strong loyalties to both Chrysler and its employees. They viewed the company positively. However, they viewed the merger negatively and faced the dilemma of leaving a company they loved versus staying and facing termination at the hands of a new executive team if they stayed.

One explanation is that many acquiring firms inadvertently alienate executives through their actions—for example, by failing to communicate effectively with the acquired top management team after the acquisition is

Acquirer's Evaluation of Acquisition

		Positive	Negative
Executive's Evaluation of Acquisition	Positive	Executive Stays A	Executive Is Fired B • Poor Performance
	Positive or Negative	Executive Quits C • Higher Status • Higher Salary • Power	Executive Quits D • Low Status • Lost Autonomy • Cultural Conflict
	Positive or Negative	Executive Quits E • Family Reasons • Spouse	Executive Quits F • Retirement • Health

Figure 9.5. Identifying poor performers

announced. Communications are often the most effective means of winning the cooperation of acquired executives and minimizing resistance to the merger. Many executives may be valuable to the new firm as it attempts to integrate the two companies. In the case of the Daimler-Chrysler merger, Chrysler's executives were subjected to a hostile work environment that had more to do with a battle for control than with the performance of individual executives. In these instances, both good and bad performers may resign. Good performers may be the first to leave as they are more likely to have outside opportunities. It is easy for acquiring firms to feel a sense of superiority following an acquisition. However, doing so almost always alienates target company executives and employees. It is difficult to integrate a firm when a firm's employees don't want to be integrated.

Another problem is that accounting performance indicators are not always good indicators of good or bad management. Firms perform poorly for a variety of reasons, including bad management, more intense competition, competition from new competitors, escalating costs, industry maturity, emerging technologies, global competition, and economic recession, among other factors. Top management teams are composed of executives with very different backgrounds, experiences, and capabilities. Executives often have wide latitude to make strategic decisions that affect the division under their charge. Decisions are often made without first gaining the approval of the firm's chief executive officer (CEO) or board. Therefore, decisions are also often distinct from the decisions of other executives who direct the activities of their own groups. Moreover, a firm's top management team is likely to include executives with varying degrees of abilities and achievements—some may be good performers while others may be bad performers. It is important for acquiring firms to assess each executive based on his or her unique capabilities rather than assigning blame to the entire top management team when firm performance falters.

Last, leadership continuity is an important determinant of organizational success. Acquiring firms may determine that an executive is undesirable and should be replaced. However, it may be necessary to keep the executive in place until a more competent executive can be found as a replacement. It takes time for new executives to learn their jobs and develop enough firm- and industry-level expertise to perform their jobs effectively. Therefore, acquirers need to balance the potentially harmful effects on organizational morale from keeping an unhappy or incompetent executive in place with the positive effects of giving the new executive sufficient time to learn his or her job.

Step 2: Keeping Good Performers

Acquiring firms must also identify and retain the most talented target executives, especially those with key skills and capabilities that support integration efforts. These executives generally fit into Cell A and Cell C in Figure 9.6. Executives in Cell A are happy with their status after the acquisition and don't consider leaving. Executives in Cell C, however, may leave to take advantage of outside opportunities. Their departure has undesirable effects on target company performance. Therefore, it is important to take steps to minimize the departure of these executives.

Successful executives may begin to analyze the costs and benefits of staying even before the acquisition has occurred. Because acquisition outcomes are uncertain, executives may make their potential availability known to outside contacts early in the acquisition process. As a result, they may be in a position to leave more quickly if they are unhappy with

Acquirer's Evaluation of Acquisition

		Positive	Negative
Executive's Evaluation of Acquisi-	Positive	Executive Stays A	Executive Is Fired B • Poor Performance
	Positive or Negative	Executive Quits C • Higher Status • Higher Salary • Job Title	Executive Quits D • Low Status • Lost Autonomy • Cultural Conflict
	Positive or Negative	Executive Quits E • Family Reasons • Spouse	Executive Quits F • Retirement • Health

Figure 9.6. Retaining top performers

their new role in the postmerger organization. Data show that executives with the best performance histories are the ones who depart the earliest.[3]

Executives respond differently to an acquisition based on the performance of the acquirer. If the acquirer is a poor performer in its industry, top executives from the acquired company are more likely to depart shortly after the acquisition. If the acquirer is a top performer in its industry, many target executives—including most poor performers—tend to stay. In these cases, turnover is more likely to appear in the second year after the acquisition, when the acquirer replaces poor performers.

Many acquiring firms spend at least 1 year evaluating target company executives before deciding which executives should be replaced or retained. This suggests a troubling picture for poor-performing acquiring firms. Many of the target company's top executives are likely to depart shortly after the acquisition. It is the target's poor performers who stay, primarily because they don't have opportunities to leave. A different picture exists for high-performing acquiring firms. Both good and bad performers prefer to stay when their firm is acquired by a high performer.

Acquiring firms that wait until the second or third year after the acquisition before making decisions about how to handle target company executives significantly reduce the potential for improving target company performance. Most importantly, the best target executives may already have left. Even in the case of acquisitions by high-performing acquiring firms, many talented executives may leave if the acquirer fails to take steps to win their cooperation and commitment. Before acquisition, target company executives hold positions at the top of their organizations. They typically have high status. After the acquisition, target company executives are forced to report to a new management team. Many executives experience a sense of lost independence and discretion. Acquiring firms may fail to notice such feelings. As a result, even good performers may think about leaving.

How do acquiring firms retain the most talented target company executives? The work of Hambrick and Cannella, which was discussed in chapter 8, provides good insight into the causes of executive turnover in target companies.[4] The primary cause of an executive's decision to quit is his or her perceived status after the acquisition. When executives are given higher status, for example, when they are given higher-level positions with greater titular status, they are less likely to depart. Granting titular status appears to be equally important to individual executives as actual job responsibilities. Greater titular status is a symbolic demonstration of the acquiring firm's recognition that the executive is an important member of the new company's dominant coalition.

Step 3: Minimizing the Effects of Unavoidable Turnover

The last step is to effectively manage the loss of executives whose departures are unavoidable (Figure 9.7). Some of these executives are good performers. Their departure can be expected to negatively affect performance. Some of these executives may also be poor performers. Their departure may be less worrisome. Nevertheless, the departure of these executives may still have negative repercussions for the firm because they disrupt ongoing projects. There is little evidence that replacement executives are any more effective than the executives they replace. Therefore, firms need to carefully assess how they manage these departures—even in cases where the acquiring firm is happy to see executives go.

Is it even possible to identify executives who might leave for unavoidable reasons such as family or health issues? If firms are able to identify

Acquirer's Evaluation of Acquisition

		Positive	Negative
Executive's Evaluation of Acquisition	Positive	Executive Stays A	Executive Is Fired B • Poor Performance
	Positive or Negative	Executive Quits C • Higher Status • Higher Salary • Job Title	Executive Quits D • Low Status • Lost Autonomy • Cultural Conflict
	Positive or Negative	Executive Quits E • Family Reasons • Spouse	Executive Quits F • Retirement • Health

Figure 9.7. Recovering from unavoidable turnover

these executives before they announce their departure, they are in a better position to begin training and socializing replacements before these executives leave. An executive who has had time to integrate him or herself into the target's culture is in a much better position to more quickly manage the responsibilities of his or her new job. Slowly transitioning new executives into vacant positions minimizes disruptions to the strategic continuity of ongoing projects. In many cases, however, an executive's decision to quit comes unexpectedly, for example when a spouse decides to relocate or when a health problem unexpectedly emerges. In these cases, it may be possible for the acquirer to negotiate a favorable package that keeps the executive in his or her position for several months until a replacement executive can be brought on board.

Conclusion

Several final issues are worth noting. Each issue affects the contribution of target company executives to the merger: (a) top management team complementarity, (b) executive tenure, and (c) management transfers.

Top Management Team Complementarity

Even when executives are good performers, there may be instances where terminating executive positions is a beneficial strategy for creating greater synergies. Hema Krishnan (Xavier University), Alex Miller (University of Tennessee), and William Judge (Old Dominion University) examined the concept of top management team complementarity—differences in functional backgrounds between the acquiring and acquired firm executives.[5] Like the concepts of strategic and organizational fit, top management team complementarity considers the potential for creating greater synergies when there is a good "fit" between the backgrounds of the two merging executive teams.

In the case of strategic and organizational fit, "fit" exists when merging firms have similar resources and common value-chain activities. Commonalities create opportunities to eliminate redundant assets that lead to scale and scope efficiencies. They also make it easier to transfer capabilities between firms, since executives in both firms have overlapping skills. In addition to synergy creation, commonalities between merging firms may mitigate cultural differences, thereby improving communication, cooperation, and shared understandings. This is associated with better performance.[6]

In contrast, top management team complementarities imply differences in functional backgrounds and skills that offset each other. Therefore, functional weaknesses in one firm's top management team are offset by functional strengths in the other firm's top management team. When merging firms have complementarities in functional skills, there are fewer redundancies that might be eliminated to lower costs. Instead, complementarity increases retention of those target company executives whose skills and backgrounds complement the skills and backgrounds of executives in the acquiring firm. Top management team complementarity is also associated with greater postmerger performance, since complementary skills are more easily integrated. In such cases, retaining key target company executives leads to improved performance.

Executive Tenure

One of the vexing problems for acquiring companies is determining which executives will leave and which executives they should try hardest to retain. One of the most important factors in determining an executive's success in an organization is his or her tenure. Executives with greater tenure develop strong firm- and industry-specific knowledge that enhances their value to the firm. Research by Donald Bergh (University of Denver) shows that retaining target company executives with longer organizational tenures leads to more successful acquisitions.[7] Moreover, retaining more senior executives decreases the probability that the acquired firm will be divested several years later.

As an executive's tenure with his or her firm increases, he or she develops idiosyncratic and nontransferable knowledge of the firm's history and culture. In addition, he or she develops relationships with suppliers, buyers, and competitors that lead to more effective strategy execution. Thus, more tenured executives are likely to possess greater leadership skills that promote effective integration and strategic continuity after the acquisition. Less tenured executives, because they have not established either knowledge of the firm or relationships with the firm's stakeholders, are less likely to be able to steer a firm through a complex acquisition integration process. Retaining more tenured executives not only keeps the wisdom and knowledge of these executives within the firm. It also sends a symbolic message to employees and shareholders that the acquiring firm values these executives' leadership abilities and the ongoing strategies of the acquired firm. Such a message is an instrumental tool for promoting cooperation and employment commitment to the newly merged firm.

Bergh's research found that retaining more tenured executives leads to greater acquisition success and retention of the acquired company over the long term. His findings suggest that acquiring firms can increase chances of acquisition success by focusing on the retention of the target company's longest tenured executives.

Management Transfers as a Strategy
for Training Future Executives

When PepsiCo transferred me to its Kentucky Fried Chicken (KFC) International Division 2 years after the KFC acquisition, I was surprised at the turmoil and animosity that continued to exist between PepsiCo and KFC executives and employees. PepsiCo regularly transferred its managers and executives among its subsidiaries (Pepsi-Cola, Frito-Lay, KFC, Taco Bell, and Pizza Hut) as a means of developing future executives. Executives rotated among subsidiaries on 2-year assignments. It became apparent to me very quickly that these transfers were one of the primary reasons why there continued to be such turmoil in KFC.

When executives are transferred into a new position, especially when they are transferred to a different division in another geographic location, it is natural that they will take actions that highlight their managerial capabilities and improve their future opportunities for promotion. At KFC, I observed a number of "restructurings" that appeared to be less effective in improving the performance of KFC than highlighting the leadership qualities of individual executives. These restructurings were accompanied by additional terminations of KFC employees, presumably to lower costs. These restructurings increased the workload of those who stayed. They also intensified the anxiety of those employees who stayed.

Management rotations may be a useful tool for promoting executive development in many cases. However, they can also create an atmosphere of continuous change that exacerbates anxieties and uncertainties among target company employees. There is strong evidence that acquisitions are rarely successful as a result of employee reductions. Exactly the opposite, acquisitions that are most successful promote the growth and performance of the target firm. Growth stimulates job opportunities and improves employee morale and commitment to the organization.

After 11 years of ownership and declining profitability, PepsiCo divested its restaurants in 1997. These restaurants—now part of Yum! Brands, Inc.—have excelled since the divestiture. The new company was located in KFC's corporate headquarters in Louisville, Kentucky. One of the first steps taken by David Novak as president and CEO was to change the sign in front of corporate headquarters to read "Franchise Support

Center." He hammered home the theme that the primary role of corporate staff would be to support the firm's franchisees and make them more profitable. The results were dramatic. Franchisee morale and company profitability increased simultaneously.

Conclusion

More than one-half of all mergers and acquisitions fail. Poor strategic fit is often a source of failure when an acquiring firm pays a high premium to acquire a firm in an unrelated industry. Few synergies can be achieved when merging firms have few commonalities in their value chains. Poor organizational and cultural fit is also a source of failure because it hinders the integration process. It creates communication costs and increases conflict. This increases the costs of integration and makes it more difficult to win the cooperation and support of target firm executives and employees.

The way in which acquiring firms manage a target company's top management team is also a source of failure in many acquisitions. Executives are important organizational resources. They are often a primary motivation of the acquisition—to acquire target company top management skills and capabilities. Few acquiring firms, however, give sufficient thought to how an effective top management team can be created after the acquisition is completed. Leadership continuity is an important determinant of acquisition success. It supports ongoing strategic projects, keeps firm- and industry-specific knowledge of key executives within the firm, and maintains an important buffer between the acquiring firm's executive team and target company employees. Target executives play an important role helping to minimize the negative psychological effects of the acquisition on employee morale and productivity.

In sum, acquisitions can be tumultuous for target company executives. A large portion of them leave shortly after acquisition. However, they are often an important determinant of acquisition success. Acquiring companies increase their chances of success when they are able to identify and retain key executives, identify and replace poor performers and executives who resist integration efforts, minimize disruptions to ongoing strategic projects, and quickly reestablish leadership continuity in the new firm.

Notes

Chapter 1

1. Collins (2001).
2. Chandler (1962).
3. Carpenter and Sanders (2008).
4. *Standard & Poor's Register of Corporations, Directors and Executives.* Charlottesville, VA: The McGraw-Hill Companies, Inc.
5. Walsh (1988).
6. *Standard & Poor's Stock Guide.* New York, NY: The McGraw-Hill Companies, Inc.
7. Walsh (1989).
8. Walsh and Ellwood (1991).
9. Walsh (1988).
10. Hambrick and Cannella (1993).
11. Krishnan, Miller, and Judge (1997).
12. Lubatkin, Schweiger, and Weber (1999).
13. SDC Platinum Database. New York: Thomson Reuters.

Chapter 2

1. SDC Platinum Database. New York: Thomson Reuters.
2. 2008 Annual Report, Procter & Gamble, Co., Cincinnati, OH.
3. Harrigan (1988); Lubatkin (1987); Parkhe (1993).
4. Biggadike (1979).
5. Barney (1991); Mahoney and Pandian (1992); Peteraf (1993); Teece, Pisano, and Shuen (1997).
6. 2008 Annual Report, Honda Motor Co., Ltd., Tokyo, Japan.
7. Brouthers and Brouthers (2000).
8. Karnitschnig and Rubenstein (2009).
9. Johnson and Winslow (2009).
10. Porter (1980), p. 3.
11. Bain (1956); Ravenscraft (1983).
12. Caves and Porter (1977).
13. Standard & Poor's Financial Services LLC (2009).
14. Winslow (2009).

15. Hennart and Reddy (1997); Wang and Zajac (2007).
16. Daniels, Krug, and Trevino (2007).
17. Krug and Daniels (2008).
18. Daniels, Krug, and Trevino (2007).

Chapter 3

1. For an in-depth examination of research on executive leadership, see Finkelstein, Hambrick, and Cannella (2009).
2. Finkelstein (2002).
3. Collins (2001).
4. 2008 Annual Report, Harley-Davidson, Inc., Milwaukee, WI (p. 3) and Annual Report 2008, Honda Motor Co., Ltd., Tokyo, Japan (p. 5).
5. Katzenbach and Smith (1993).
6. Hambrick, Cho, and Chen (1996); Hambrick and Mason (1984).
7. Child (1972).
8. Chandler (1991).
9. Katzenbach (1998).
10. Chandler (1962).
11. Jensen and Meckling (1976), p. 310.
12. Fama and Jensen (1983).
13. 2007 10-K Report, Merrill Lynch & Co., Inc., New York, NY. Form 10-K filed with United States Securities and Exchange Commission for fiscal year ended December 28, 2007 (p. 81).
14. 2008 10-K Report, Merrill Lynch & Co., Inc., New York, NY. Form 10-K filed with United States Securities and Exchange Commission for fiscal year ended December 28, 2008 (p. 52).
15. Fitzpatrick, Craig, and Mollenkamp (2009).
16. Kell (2009).
17. von Clausewitz (1963).
18. Schweiger and Sandberg (1989).
19. Kesner and Sebora (1994); Shen and Cannella (2002).
20. Schwartz and Menon (1985).
21. Hambrick and D'Aveni (1992).
22. Davidson, Worrell, and Cheng (1990).
23. Dooley and Fryxell (1999).

Chapter 4

1. Krug and Shill (2008).
2. Walsh and Kosnik (1993).

3. Bourgeois (1980).
4. Barney (1991).
5. Coase (1937).
6. Arrow (1974).
7. Williamson (1981).
8. Chandler (1962).
9. Simon (1957).
10. Teece (1980).
11. Williamson (1981), p. 1542.
12. Yip (1982).
13. Grant (1996).
14. Haleblian and Finkelstein (1999).
15. Zollo and Singh (2004).
16. Hitt, Hoskisson, Ireland, and Harrison (1991), p.7.
17. Bergh (2001); Porter (1987); Ravenscraft and Scherer (1987).
18. Bruner (2004).
19. Bruner (2004), p. 44.
20. King, Dalton, Daily, and Covin (2004).
21. Datta, Pinches, and Narayanan (1992); King, Dalton, Daily, and Covin (2004).

Chapter 5

1. Porter (1987).
2. Rappaport (1986).
3. Rappaport (1986), pp. 19–49.
4. Barney (1991); Grant (1991); Mahoney and Pandian (1992); Peteraf (1993).
5. *Fortune*, "The World's Most Admired Companies." (2009), pp. 75–86.
6. Kitching (1967).
7. Roll (1986).
8. Marks and Mirvis (1998); Schweiger and Goulet (2005).
9. Trautwein (1990).
10. Montgomery and Singh (1984); Rumelt (1982).
11. Berle and Means (1933).
12. Simon (1957).
13. Duhaime and Schwenk (1985).
14. Jemison and Sitkin (1986).
15. Roll (1986).
16. Bain (1959).
17. Schmalensee (1985).
18. Wernerfelt and Montgomery (1986).

Chapter 6

1. Walsh (1988).
2. Fama (1980); Fama and Jensen (1983); Jensen and Meckling (1976).
3. Jemison and Sitkin (1986).
4. Barney (1988); Castanias and Helfat (1991); Walsh and Ellwood (1991).
5. Cannella and Hambrick (1993).
6. Krishnan, Miller, and Judge (1997).

Chapter 7

1. Federal Trade Commission (1981).
2. Baker, Miller, and Ramsperger (1981).
3. Walter and Barney (1990).
4. Bower (2001).

Chapter 8

1. Halpern and Weston (1983); Jensen and Ruback (1983); Lubatkin (1983); Rappaport (1986).
2. Buono, Bowditch, and Lewis (1985); Haspeslagh and Jemison (1991); Jemison and Sitkin (1986); Marks and Mirvis (1998); Pablo, Sitkin, and Jemison (1996).
3. Jemison and Sitkin (1986).
4. Walsh (1988).
5. Hambrick and Cannella (1993).
6. Hirsch (1986).
7. Frank (1985).
8. Walsh (1989).
9. Krug and Nigh (1998).
10. Krug (2009); Krug (2003a, 2003b); Krug and Aguilera (2005); Krug and Hegarty (1997, 2001); Krug and Nigh (1998, 2001).
11. Krug and Nigh (1998).
12. Hambrick and Cannella (1993); Walsh (1989).
13. Cannella and Hambrick (1993).
14. Walsh and Kosnik (1993).
15. Jensen and Smith (1985).
16. Jensen and Meckling (1976).
17. Walsh and Ellwood (1991).
18. Walsh and Kosnik (1993).
19. Porter (1987); Rumelt (1974); Salter and Weinhold (1979).
20. King, Dalton, Daily, and Covin (2004).

21. Barney (1988); Lubatkin (1987); Montgomery and Singh (1984).
22. Capron and Pistre (2002).
23. Haspeslagh and Jemison (1991); Marks and Mirvis (1998).
24. Walsh (1988, 1989).
25. Cannella and Hambrick (1993); Hambrick and Cannella (1993).
26. Krug and Nigh (1998).
27. Kobrin (1991).

Chapter 9

1. Bluedorn (1978); Mobley (1982); Price (1976).
2. Campion (1991).
3. Walsh and Ellwood (1991).
4. Hambrick and Cannella (1993).
5. Krishnan, Miller, and Judge (1997).
6. Michel and Hambrick (1992); Wiersema and Bantel (1992).
7. Bergh (2001).

References

Abelson, M. A. (1987). Examination of avoidable and unavoidable turnover. *Journal of Applied Psychology, 72*(3), 382–386.

Arrow, K. J. (1974). *The limits of organization*. New York: W. W. Norton.

Bain, J. S. (1956). *Barriers to new competition*. Cambridge, MA: Harvard University Press.

Bain, J. S. (1959). *Industrial organization*. New York: John Wiley & Sons.

Baker, H., Kent, M., Thomas O., & Ramsperger, B. J. (1981). A typology of merger motives. *Akron Business and Law Review, 12*(4), 24–29.

Barney, J. (1988). Returns to bidding firms in mergers and acquisitions: Reconsidering the relatedness hypothesis. *Strategic Management Journal, 9*(5), 71–78.

Barney, J. (1991). Firm resources and sustained competitive advantage. *Journal of Management, 17*(1), 99–120.

Bergh, D. D. (2001). Executive retention and acquisition outcomes: A test of opposing views on the influence of organizational tenure. *Journal of Management, 27*(5), 603–622.

Berle, A. A., Jr., & Means, G. C. (1933). *The modern corporation and private property*. New York: Macmillan.

Biggadike, R. (1979). The risky business of diversification. *Harvard Business Review, 57*(3), 103–111.

Bluedorn, A. C. (1978). A taxonomy of turnover. *Academy of Management Review, 3*(3), 647–651.

Bourgeois, L. J., III. (1980). Strategy and environment: A conceptual integration. *Academy of Management Review, 5*(1), 25–39.

Bower, J. L. (2001). Not all M&As are alike—and that matters. *Harvard Business Review, 79*(3), 93–101.

Brouthers, K. D., & Brouthers, L. E. (2000). Acquisition or greenfield start-up? Institutional, cultural and transaction cost influences. *Strategic Management Journal, 21*(1), 89–97.

Bruner, R. F. (2004). *Applied mergers & acquisitions*. Hoboken, NJ: John Wiley & Sons.

Buono, A. F., Bowditch, J. L., & Lewis, J. W., III. (1985). When cultures collide: The anatomy of a merger. *Human Relations, 35*(8), 477–501.

Campion, M. A. (1991). Meaning and measurement of turnover: Comparison of alternative measures and recommendations for research. *Journal of Applied Psychology, 76*(2), 199–212.

Cannella, A. A., Jr., & Hambrick, D. C. (1993). Effects of executive departures on the performance of acquired firms. *Strategic Management Review, 14,* 137–152.

Capron, L., & Pistre, N. (2002). When do acquirers earn abnormal returns? *Strategic Management Journal, 23*(9), 781–794.

Carpenter, M. A., & Sanders, G. (2008). *Strategic management.* New York: Prentice Hall.

Castanias, R. P., & Helfat, C. E. (1991). Managerial resources and rents. *Journal of Management, 17*(1), 155–171.

Caves, R. E., & Porter, M. E. (1977). From entry barriers to mobility barriers: Conjectural decisions and contrived deterrence to new competition. *Quarterly Journal of Economics, 91*(2), 241–262.

Chandler, A. D., Jr. (1962). *Strategy and structure: Chapters in the history of the industrial enterprise.* Cambridge, MA: MIT Press.

Chandler, A. D., Jr. (1991). The functions of the HQ unit in the multibuisness firm [Special issue]. *Strategic Management Journal, 12,* 31–50.

Child, J. (1972). Organization structure, environment and performance: The role of strategic choice. *Sociology, 6*(1), 1–22.

Coase, R. (1937). The nature of the firm. *Economica, 4,* 386–405.

Collins, J. (2001). *Good to great.* New York: HarperCollins.

Dalton, D. R., Todor, W. D., & Krackhardt, D. M. (1982). Turnover overstated: The functional taxonomy. *Academy of Management Review, 7*(1), 117–123.

Daniels, J. D., Krug, J. A., & Trevino, L. (2007). Foreign direct investment from Latin America and the Caribbean. *Transnational Corporations, 16,* 27–53.

Datta, D. K., Pinches, G. E., & Narayanan, V. K. (1992). Factors influencing wealth creation from mergers and acquisitions: A meta-analysis. *Strategic Management Journal, 13*(1), 67–84.

Davidson, W. N., III, Worrell, D. L., & Cheng, L. (1990). Key executive succession and stockholder wealth: The influence of successor's origin, position, and age. *Journal of Management, 16*(3), 647–665.

Dooley, R. S., & Fryxell, G. E. (1999). Attaining decision quality and commitment from dissent: The moderating effects of loyalty and competence in strategic decision-making teams. *Academy of Management Journal, 42*(4), 389–402.

Duhaime, I. M., & Schwenk, C. R. (1985). Conjectures on cognitive simplification in acquisition and divestment decision making. *Academy of Management Review, 10*(2), 287–295.

Fama, E. F. (1980). Agency problems and the theory of the firm. *Journal of Political Economy, 88*(2), 288–307.

Fama, E. F., & Jensen, M. C. (1983). Separation of ownership and control. *Journal of Law and Economics, 26*(2), 301–325.

Federal Trade Commission. (1981). *Statistical report on mergers and acquisitions, 1979.* Washington, DC: U.S. Government Printing Office.

Finkelstein, S. (2002). *The DaimlerChrysler Merger.* Hanover, NH: Tuck School of Business, Dartmouth College, no. 1–0071.

Finkelstein, S., Hambrick, D. C., & Cannella, A. A., Jr. (2009). *Strategic leadership: Theory and research on executives, top management teams, and boards.* Oxford, UK: Oxford University Press.

Fitzpatrick, D., Craig, S., & Mollenkamp, C. (2009, January 23). Thain ousted in clash at Bank of America. *Wall Street Journal,* p. A1.

Frank, R. (1985). *Choosing the right pond: Human behavior and the quest for status.* New York: Oxford University Press.

Grant, R. M. (1991). The resource-based theory of competitive advantage: Implications for strategy formulation. *California Management Review, 33*(3), 114–135.

Grant, R. M. (1996, Winter). Toward a knowledge-based theory of the firm [Special issue]. *Strategic Management Journal, 17,* 109–122.

Haleblian, J., & Finkelstein, S. (1999). The influence of organizational acquisition experience on acquisition performance: A behavioral perspective. *Administrative Science Quarterly, 44*(1), 29–56.

Halpern, P., & Weston, J. F. (1983). Corporate acquisitions: A theory of special cases? A review of event studies applied to acquisitions. *Journal of Finance, 38*(2), 297–321.

Hambrick, D. C., & Cannella, A. A., Jr. (1993). Relative standing: A framework for understanding departures of acquired executives. *Academy of Management Journal, 36*(4), 733–762.

Hambrick, D. C., Cho, T. S., & Chen, M.-J. (1996). The influence of top management team heterogeneity on firms' competitive moves. *Administrative Science Quarterly, 41*(4), 659–684.

Hambrick, D. C., & D'Aveni, R. A. (1992). Top team deterioration as part of the downward spiral of large corporate bankruptcies. *Management Science, 38*(10), 1445–1466.

Hambrick, D. C., & Mason, P. A. (1984). Upper echelons: The organization as a reflection of its top managers. *Academy of Management Review, 9*(2), 193–206.

Harrigan, K. R. (1988). Joint ventures and competitive strategy. *Strategic Management Journal, 9*(2), 141–158.

Haspeslagh, P. C., & Jemison, D. B. (1991). The challenge of renewal through acquisitions. *Planning Review, 19*(2), 27–31.

Hennart, J.-F., & Reddy, S. (1997). The choice between mergers/acquisitions and joint ventures: The case of Japanese investors in the United States. *Strategic Management Journal, 18*(1), 1–12.

Hirsch, P. M. (1986). From ambushes to golden parachutes: Corporate takeovers as an instance of cultural framing and institutional integration. *American Journal of Sociology,* 91, 800–837.

Hitt, M. A., Hoskisson, R. E., Ireland, R. D., & Harrison, J. S. (1991). Effects of acquisitions on R&D inputs and outputs. *Academy of Management Journal, 34*(3), 693–706.

Jemison, D. B., & Sitkin, S. B. (1986). Corporate acquisitions: A process perspective. *Academy of Management Review, 14*(1), 145–163.

Jensen, M. C., & Meckling, W. H. (1976). Theory of the firm: Managerial behavior, agency costs and ownership structure. *Journal of Financial Economics, 3*(4), 305–360.

Jensen, M. C., & Ruback, R. S. (1983). The market for corporate control: The scientific evidence. *Journal of Financial Economics, 11*(1), 5–50.

Jensen, M. C., & Smith, C. (1985). Stockholder, manager, and creditor interests: Applications of agency theory. In E. I. Altman and M. G. Subrahmanyam (Eds.), *Recent advances in corporate finance* (pp. 95–131). Homewood, IL: Richard D. Irwin.

Johnson, A., & Winslow, R. (2009, March 10). Drug-industry shakeout hits small firms hard—Another wave of acquisitions is likely as companies worry about their drug pipelines and health-care change. *Wall Street Journal,* p. A12.

Karnitschnig, M., & Rubenstein, S. (2009, January 24). Pfizer nears giant drug deal. *Wall Street Journal,* p. A1.

Katzenbach, J. R. (1998). *Teams at the top.* Boston: Harvard Business School Press.

Katzenbach, J. R., & Smith, D. (1993). *The wisdom of teams.* Boston: Harvard Business School Press.

Kell, J. (2009, February 17). Bank of America makes $401M TARP payment to U.S. government. *Dow Jones Newswires,* p. A1.

Kesner, I. F., & Sebora, T. C. (1994). Executive succession: Past, present & future. *Journal of Management, 20*(2), 327–376.

King, D. R., Dalton, D. R., Daily, C. M., & Covin, J. G. (2004). Meta-analyses of post-acquisition performance: Indications of unidentified moderators. *Strategic Management Journal, 25*(2), 187–200.

Kitching, J. (1967). Why do mergers miscarry? *Harvard Business Review,* 45, 84–101.

Kobrin, S. J. (1991). An empirical analysis of the determinants of global integration. *Strategic Management Journal, 12*, 17–31.

Krishnan, H. A., Miller, A., & Judge, W. Q. (1997). Diversification and top management team complementarity: Is performance improved by merging similar or dissimilar teams? *Strategic Management Journal, 18*(5), 361–374.

Krug, J. A. (2003a). Executive turnover in acquired firms: An analysis of resource-based theory and the upper echelons perspective. *Journal of Management & Governance, 7*(2), 117–143.

Krug, J. A. (2003b). Why do they keep leaving? *Harvard Business Review, 81*, 14–15.

Krug, J. A. (2009). Brain drain: Why top management bolts after M&As. *Journal of Business Strategy, 30*, 4–14.

Krug, J. A., & Aguilera, R. V. (2005). Top management team turnover in mergers and acquisitions. In C. L. Cooper & S. Finkelstein (Eds.), *Advances in mergers & acquisitions, 4*, 123–154.

Krug, J. A., & Daniels, J. D. (Eds.). (2008). *Multinational enterprise theory.* London: Sage Publications.

Krug, J. A., & Hegarty, W. H. (1997). Postacquisition turnover among U.S. top management teams: An analysis of the effects of foreign versus domestic acquisitions of U.S. targets. *Strategic Management Journal, 18*(8), 667–675.

Krug, J. A., & Hegarty, W. H. (2001). Predicting who stays and leaves after an acquisition: A study of top managers in multinational firms. *Strategic Management Journal, 22*(2), 185–196.

Krug, J. A., & Nigh, D. (1998). Top management departures in cross-border acquisitions: Governance issues in an international context. *Journal of International Management, 4*, 267–287.

Krug, J. A., & Nigh, D. (2001). Executive perceptions in foreign and domestic acquisitions: An analysis of foreign ownership and its effect on executive fate. *Journal of World Business, 36*(1), 85–105.

Krug, J. A., & Shill, W. (2008). The big exit: Executive churn in the wake of M&As. *Journal of Business Strategy, 29*(4), 15–21.

Lubatkin, M. (1983). Mergers and performance of the acquiring firm. *Academy of Management Review, 8*(2), 218–225.

Lubatkin, M. (1987). Merger strategies and stockholder value. *Strategic Management Journal, 8*(1), 39–53.

Lubatkin, M., Schweiger, D. M., & Weber, Y. (1999). Top management turnover in related M&As: An additional test of the theory of relative standing. *Journal of Management, 25*, 55–73.

Mahoney, J. T., & Pandian, R. J. (1992). The resource-based view within the conversation of strategic management. *Strategic Management Journal, 13*(5), 363–380.

Marks, M. L., & Mirvis, P. H. (1998). *Joining forces: Making one plus one equal three in mergers, acquisitions, and alliances.* San Francisco: Jossey-Bass.

Michel, J. G., & Hambrick, D. C. (1992). Diversification posture and top management team characteristics. *Academy of Management Journal, 35*(1), 9–37.

Mobley, W. H. (1982). *Employee turnover: Causes, consequences and control.* Reading, MA: Addison-Wesley.

Montgomery, C. A., & Singh, H. (1984). Diversification strategy and systematic risk. *Strategic Management Journal, 5*(2), 181–191.

Pablo, A. L., Sitkin, S. B., & Jemison, D. B. (1996). Acquisition decision-making processes: The central role of risk. *Journal of Management, 22*(5), 723–746.

Parkhe, A. (1993). Strategic alliance structuring: A game theoretic and transaction cost examination of interfirm cooperation. *Academy of Management Journal, 36*(4), 794–829.

Peteraf, M. A. (1993). The cornerstones of competitive advantage: A resource-based view. *Strategic Management Journal, 14*(3), 179–191.

Porter, M. E. (1980). *Competitive strategy: Techniques for analyzing industries and competitors.* New York: The Free Press.

Porter, M. E. (1987). From competitive advantage to corporate strategy. *Harvard Business Review, 65*(3), 43–59.

Price, J. L. (1976). The measurement of turnover. *Industrial Relations, 6*, 33–46.

Rappaort, A. (1986). *Creating shareholder value.* New York: The Free Press.

Ravenscraft, D. J. (1983). Structure-profit relationship at the line of business and industry level. *Review of Economics and Statistics, 61*(1), 22–31.

Ravenscraft, D. J., & Scherer, F. M. (1987). *Mergers, sell-offs, and economic efficiency.* Washington, DC: Brookings.

Roll, R. (1986). The hubris hypothesis of corporate takeovers. *Journal of Business, 59*(2), 197–216.

Rumelt, R. P. (1974). *Strategy, structure, and economic performance.* Boston: Harvard University Press.

Rumelt, R. P. (1982). Diversification strategy and profitability. *Strategic Management Journal, 3*(4), 359–369.

Salter, M. S., & Weinhold, W. A. (1979). *Diversification through acquisition: Strategies for maximizing economic value.* New York: The Free Press.

Schmalensee, R. (1985). Do markets differ much? *American Economic Review, 75*(3), 341–351.

Schwartz, K. B., & Menon, K. (1985). Executive succession in failing firms. *Academy of Management Journal, 28*(3), 680–697.

Schweiger, D. M., & Goulet, P. K. (2005). Facilitating acquisitions integration through deep-level cultural learning interventions: A longitudinal field experiment. *Organization Studies, 26*(10), 1477–1499.

Schweiger, D. M., & Sandberg, W. R. (1989). The utilization of individual capabilities in group approaches to strategic decisionmaking. *Strategic Management Journal, 10*(1), 31–43.

Shen, W., & Cannella, A. A., Jr. (2002). Power dynamics within top management and their impact on CEO dismissal followed by inside succession. *Academy of Management Journal, 45*(6), 1195–1206.

Simon, H. A. (1957). *Administrative behavior: A study of decision-making processes in administrative organization.* New York: Macmillan.

Teece, D. J. (1980). Economies of scope and the scope of the enterprise. *Journal of Economic Behavior and Organization, 1,* 223–247.

Teece, D. J., Pisano, G., & Shuen, A. (1997). Dynamic capabilities and strategic management. *Strategic Management Journal, 18*(7), 509–533.

Trautwein, F. (1990). Merger motives and merger prescriptions. *Strategic Management Journal, 11*(4), 283–295.

von Clausewitz, C.. (1963). *Vom Kriege.* Hamburg: Rowohlt Taschenbuch Verlag.

Walsh, J. P. (1988). Top management turnover following mergers and acquisitions. *Strategic Management Journal, 9*(2), 173–183.

Walsh, J. P. (1989). Doing a deal: Merger and acquisition negotiations and their impact upon target company top management turnover. *Strategic Management Journal, 10*(4), 307–322.

Walsh, J. P., & Ellwood, J. W. (1991). Mergers, acquisitions, and the pruning of managerial deadwood: An examination of the market for corporate control. *Strategic Management Journal, 12*(3), 201–217.

Walsh, J. P., & Kosnik, R. D. (1993). Corporate raiders and their disciplinary role in the market. *Academy of Management Journal, 36*(4), 671–700.

Walter, G. A., & Barney, J. B. (1990). Management objectives in mergers and acquisitions. *Strategic Management Journal, 11*(1), 79–86.

Wang, L., & Zajac, E. J. (2007). Alliance or acquisition? A dyadic perspective on interfirm resource combinations. *Strategic Management Journal, 28*(13), 1291–1347.

Wernerfelt, B., & Montgomery, C. A. (1986). What is an attractive industry? *Management Science, 32*(10), 1223–1230.

Wiersema, M. F., & Bantel, K. A. (1992). Top management team demography and corporate strategic change. *Academy of Management Journal, 35*(1), 91–121.

Williamson, O. E. (1981). The modern corporation: Origins, evolution, attributes. *Journal of Economic Literature, 19,* 1537–1568.

Winslow, R. (2009, January 27). Pfizer sets $2.3 billion settlement—agreement with U.S. tied to alleged off-label marketing of painkiller Bextra. *Wall Street Journal,* p. B2.

The world's most admired companies 2009. (2009, March 16). *Fortune,* pp. 75–88.

Yip, G. S. (1982). Diversification entry: Internal development versus acquisition. *Strategic Management Journal, 3*(4), 331–345.

Zollo, M., & Singh, H. (2004). Deliberate learning in corporate acquisitions: Post-acquisition strategies and integration capability in U.S. bank mergers. *Strategic Management Journal, 25*(13), 1233–1256.

Index

Note: The italicized *f* or *t* following page numbers refers to figures or tables, respectively.